TIMBRE 4
TWO PLAYS BY CLAUDIO TOLCACHIR

TIMBRE 4
TWO PLAYS BY CLAUDIO TOLCACHIR

EDITED
BY
JEAN GRAHAM-JONES

TRANSLATED
BY
JEAN GRAHAM-JONES AND ELISA LEGON

MARTIN E. SEGAL THEATRE CENTER PUBLICATIONS
NEW YORK

Timbre 4: Two Plays by Claudio Tolcachir

Library of Congress Cataloging-in-Publication Data

Tolcachir, Claudio, 1975-
  [Omisión de la familia Coleman. English]
  Timbre 4 : 2 plays / by Claudio Tolcachir ; edited by Jean Graham-Jones ; translated by Jean Graham-Jones and Elisa Legon.
    p. cm.
  ISBN 978-0-9846160-0-8
  I. Graham-Jones, Jean. II. Tolcachir, Claudio, 1975- Tercer cuerpo. English. III. Title.
  PQ7798.43.O53O4513 2010
  862'.7--dc22
                    2010035992

This Martin E. Segal Theatre Center Publications book was published within the framework of the 'Sur' Translation Support Program of the Ministry of Foreign Affairs, International Trade and Worship of the Argentine Republic.

La omisión de la familia Coleman © 2008 by Claudio Tolcachir, translation copyright © 2010 by Elisa Legon and Jean Graham-Jones; Tercer cuerpo © 2008 by Claudio Tolcachir, translation copyright © 2010 by Jean Graham-Jones.

Copy-editing, typography, and design: Gad Guterman
Cover photograph: Giampaolo Samà/Timbre 4
Translation review: Adam Versényi

© 2010 Martin E. Segal Theatre Center
Daniel Gerould, Director of Publications
Frank Hentschker, Executive Director
Jan Stenzel, Director of Administration

TIMBRE 4
TWO PLAYS BY CLAUDIO TOLCACHIR

TABLE OF CONTENTS

Photo by Giampaolo Samà/Timbre 4

Introduction:
"The Irresistible Rise of Claudio Tolcachir and Timbre 4"

Even by the remarkable standards of Buenos Aires's current vibrant, vital theatre scene, the success of Timbre 4 and its director, Claudio Tolcachir, stands out. In many ways the company's two major productions—*La omisión de la familia Coleman* and *Tercer cuerpo (la historia de un intento absurdo)*, both appearing here in their first English-language translation—exemplify the Argentinean capital's longtime institution of what is known locally as "independent theatre": a tradition of non-commercial, non-state supported, sociopolitically engaged, and aesthetically experimental theatre dating back to the 1930s. Today the independent theatre, often referred to as "Off" (in rough analogy to New York's Off-Off-Broadway scene), constitutes Buenos Aires's most active theatrical circuit, with over 300 small theatres scattered throughout the city and with performances taking place in plazas and streets, on buses and subways, converted warehouses and houses, and even in living rooms of private dwellings. Timbre 4, like so many of its independent peers, maintains a fluid programming that allows for long rehearsal periods and extended multiyear runs. After premiering in 2005, its first major production (*La omisión de la familia Coleman*) nears 1,000 performances as it still runs on weekends; and its second production (*Tercer cuerpo*), premiered in 2008, recently celebrated its 300th performance. Local critical and public response to both productions has been overwhelming: the author/director, actors, texts, designers, and productions have received Buenos Aires's major awards, tickets often sell out weeks in advance, and spectators overflowing the risers can find themselves seated in any available onstage chair. At the same time Timbre 4 has achieved international acclaim. The company has been featured at nearly all the major United States Latina/o, Latin American, and European theatre festivals; and its productions have had multiple-season sell-out extended runs in some of Spain's major theatres. The phenomenon that is Timbre 4 stands as a fascinating case of theatre's survival in today's increasingly complex network of the local and global.

It all started in a small house in Buenos Aires's historically working-class, now ever-more gentrified, neighborhood of Boedo. Timbre 4's name comes from the buzzer to what was once Tolcachir's residence at the back of a *casa chorizo*, a descriptive term for the sausage-string layout created when traditional houses were subdivided to accommodate the city's swelling early-twentieth-century immigrant population. To arrive at the fifty-seat theatre, one walked down a private passageway leading to a shared internal patio. The performance space occupied a large room, and the entry door and casement windows looking out onto the courtyard (and, beside it, a separate bathroom) formed the playing space's upstage wall. Mentioned in nearly every critical account of a Timbre 4 performance, the theatre's location has played a key role in the company's identity. This is how Timbre 4 tells its own story:

> Timbre 4 is a house. And the house is a school. And the school is a theatre. Let's try this again. Timbre 4 is found at the end of a long hallway in a casa chorizo.
> There are neighbors. And, yes, in the last house there lives a theatre director who gives acting classes. Yes, right there. No, not at home, exactly... Let's try this again.
>
> In this house, at the end of a long hallway there lives a theatre director who, yes, it's true, also writes, he's a playwright, yes. And, yes, he gives classes there. At home... More or less. Very nearby, how about that. In his school. Yes, in Timbre 4. The green door at the end. No, sorry. If you want tickets for the theatre, the box office is the other door, the red one. Yes, this is a theatre, yes. Come on in. Welcome.[1]

The company's success and neighborhood location have not been without problems: for instance, theatregoers warned against talking while moving down 640 Boedo Avenue's hall nevertheless incurred the wrath of one neighbor, who accused the company of prostitution and drug-trafficking. Indeed, the ongoing conflict forced Timbre 4 to find an independent entry to its theatre. This search resulted in the company's occupying an old chair factory that shares the back wall of Tolcachir's apartment, all of which will eventually be accessible through a shared hallway. Yet even in its larger 180-seat space on México Street, opened in June 2010, Timbre 4 remains a neighborhood theatre.

Claudio Tolcachir is himself a home-grown product of Buenos Aires. Born in 1975, "Tolca"—as he is known in the local theatre community—has led a life in the city's theatre for over twenty years. He began at the age of sixteen, as a student of and assistant to legendary actress and director Alejandra Boero, one of the founders of Buenos Aires's independent theatre movement. Studies at the Labardén Vocational Art Institute provided a broad artistic background, enhanced by growing up with a brother who is today an orchestral conductor and a father who began to study acting while his son was an adolescent. Tolcachir has built an extensive résumé as a stage actor on the independent and commercial theatre scenes, working with some of the city's leading directors—including Daniel Veronese, Luciano Suardi, Agustín Alezzo, Roberto Villanueva, José María Paoloantonio, and Norma Aleandro—and making sporadic incursions into film and television.

He still performs, often finding himself acting in other Buenos Aires shows while writing, rehearsing, and producing his own plays. Known for his blond good looks, charismatic stage presence, agile physicality, and total emotional commitment, Tolcachir has admitted, "When I don't act for a while, I begin to go a little bit crazy."[2] In recent years, in addition to staging his own plays in his own space, he has made an impact on Buenos Aires's commercial theatre scene with hit productions of two US plays: Tracy Lett's *August: Osage County* and Arthur Miller's *All My Sons*. Tolcachir's directing star continues to rise.

Tolcachir's Timbre 4 is also a private acting school, with seventeen teachers, many of whom act, write, and now stage their own productions. In the late 1990s Tolcachir—like many Buenos Aires theatre artists—opened his Boedo home as a studio, where, building upon Timbre 4's actor training program, he began to stage his own productions. These early projects were primarily adaptations of previous texts, including Argentinean dramatist Roberto Arlt's famous 1930s play *300 millones* (300 Million), a version which Tolcachir premiered as *Jamón del Diablo* (Devilled Ham or Spam) in 2002. The production ran for four years and some 300 performances.

It was in this studio-home that Tolcachir created his first original play, *La omisión de la familia Coleman* (The Coleman Family's Omission), often abbreviated locally as *Coleman*. The text was developed with the actors over nine months of rehearsals through what Tolcachir has described as "writing in movement": "The working process was carried out through improvisations and composition exercises with the characters, their traits, and their bonds, gradually arriving at the idea of the definitive text."[3] Tolcachir asked the actors not to seek immediate dramatic conflict but first to develop their individual characters and then the relationships among them without forcing the situations.[4] Logistical necessity drove other dramaturgical decisions: for example, when an actor's job kept her away from the Boedo theatre, the company rehearsed by telephone and eventually incorporated the phone call into the text. The resulting two-act play in many ways combines what in Buenos Aires is called an "actor's text" with the traditional "playwright's text," creating a work rich in extreme characterization and hallucinatory in its rhythms and whirls. In August 2005 the production opened in Tolcachir's old home in a conscious fusion of theatre and life: "The audience enters the room by crossing the family's set, creating the sensation that they're inside this house, inside this world. The space is realistic, with details that tell us of this family's personality, its accumulation of objects and overlapping of styles."[5] As one review noted, the "peeling wallpaper, shabby and mismatched furniture, and original architectural details" became part of the performance.[6] With the fifty spectators mere inches away from the action, the intimacy of the space and the depth of character development culminated in an intensely experienced theatrical event.

In many ways the six-member Coleman family resembles earlier Argentine theatrical households. Like the families typical of the River Plate region's twentieth-century theatrical grotesque tradition, the Colemans are both over the top and completely recognizable; they inspire repulsion and empathy, laughter and discomfort. Their precarious lifestyle echoes the trials of today's post-crash Argentina facing few prospects, and Timbre 4's falling-apart house stands for much more than a struggling theatre company, as we witness a family unraveling at its seams. There is no patriarch, and the aging and ill grandmother, Leonarda, is not up to the task of holding the family together. Her daughter, Memé, arrested in a state of perpetual adolescence, refuses to take responsibility for herself or for her four now-adult children. It thus falls to her daughter Gabi to attempt to support the family by repairing used clothing and reselling it at a flea market. Gabi's twin brother, Damián, is a substance-using petty thief who furtively enters and exits the family dwelling in search of his own survival. Memé's unsettlingly close relationship with her other son, Marito, has apparently contributed to his troubles, some of which may be permanent and only occasionally offset by his strange prescience. Only Verónica, Memé's other daughter, has apparently escaped the family's web, raised by her father (who abandoned his son Marito to be raised by Memé) and now married into wealth with two children of her own. When Leonarda is taken to a hospital (indicated by a simple yet effective shift in lights and set), Verónica is drawn back into the family. After Leonarda's death, the tenuous family unit is finally exploded, leaving Marito alone—unaware that he has been diagnosed with leukemia—waiting vainly for his family to return as the audience listens to Argentinean singer Violeta Rivas's recorded voice: "How lucky I am to have such a good mother…"

While at first glance clearly dysfunctional, the Coleman family is also disconcertingly "normal." Argentinean playwright Mauricio Kartun notes: "The Colemans, in their exquisite equilibrium, in their prehistoric wisdom, become in today's society (and every society) the most accomplished, condemning, and perfect image of functionality."[7] Dysfunctionality has in fact become the only means by which families can survive the ravages of free-market capitalism in a world turned upside down. Yet, despite the universality of the Colemans' plight, the play is grounded in Timbre 4's Boedo neighborhood. Local slang carves out generational and class divisions within the family, just as the bathroom's broken faucets remind audiences that what they're witnessing is not entirely fictional.

Ultimately, the play's title reminds us, the Coleman family is complicit in its own demise. Not only do they seem to have been overlooked by society, they themselves have sinned by omission: mysteriously absent fathers, outrageously irresponsible mothers, hypocrisy, parasitism, and violence corrode the family. As Macarena Trigo writes in her extended study, "[O]mission is converted into a way of life, a survival strategy. If we avoid everything that bothers us, perhaps it will disappear. This seems to be the implied hope."[8] Self-imposed silencing and the lack of communication appear to be the greatest sins. The cost is the destruction of the family, the presumed bedrock of any society.

Tercer cuerpo, Tolcachir's second play, moves outside the family residence and into the social sphere of the workplace. Written, the author notes, "in airports" during a *Coleman* international tour, the play exhibits a completely different structure and focus even though its plot similarly turns on what characters leave unsaid or hidden. The play's main action takes place in an abandoned wing of an office building, where three coworkers attempt to carry out apparently obsolete tasks. Tolcachir describes the location as "an office that doesn't have any more reason for being, its services have no meaning. The characters are halfway through their lives, and they don't have any reason for being either. In reality, they have an enormous need to love. They don't say the truth about what's going on because they're ashamed of themselves."[9] Multiple spaces coexist in this public-as-private sphere: without modifying the basic office set, characters appear in restaurants, bars, and their own homes; a simple shift of a chair takes a character from her office desk to a doctor's office; and at one point four different locations are presented simultaneously. The original production occupied less than half the space taken up by *Coleman*. Nestled in one corner of Timbre 4's dilapidated theatre, the contained playing area was drably furnished with ramshackle office supplies and furniture (one of the desk legs had a piece of wood shoved under it to level it out), and a wall covered the apartment's casement windows, allowing only a narrow door leading in and out. The audience, hovering around the stage, added to the claustrophobia of these five bodies occupying the same physical space but living in largely isolated worlds.

In this environment of shared solitude, we find coworkers Moni, Sandra, and Héctor. Moni, homeless, is secretly living in the office; Sandra, single, desperately wants to have a child and lies to her doctor about her non-existent husband; and Héctor has recently lost his mother and, in an apparent midlife crisis, has dyed his hair and taken up with various young men and women. Among these pickups is Manuel, who lives with Sofía in a less-than-happy relationship. All five characters desperately combat loneliness, whose presence is made even more palpable by an original staging that places the actors in suffocating proximity and heartbreaking isolation, culminating in what one reviewer called a chorale of "trio and duet" created with "admirable musical precision."[10] Perhaps more universally than in his first play, Tolcachir emphasizes the misery of contemporary life, of limited economic possibilities, and of even more limited opportunities for happiness. His characters nevertheless persevere in their "absurd attempts" (of the play's subtitle) at love in the face of fear and helplessness. The resulting work is a darkly humorous tragicomedy of minimal yet haunting proportions.

Though easily regarded as very local, very Argentinean plays, both *La omisión de la familia Coleman* and *Tercer cuerpo* have also resonated with international audiences. The two productions have played at international festivals in Bolivia, Bosnia, Brazil, Chile, Colombia, Costa Rica, El Salvador, France, Germany, Ireland, Panama, Peru, Portugal, Spain, Switzerland, and the United States. And while international audiences may see themselves reflected in both plays (Tolcachir recalls one man asking him after a *Coleman* performance in Dublin, "Did you get your inspiration from an Irish family?"), there is a captivating immediacy to each that is the product of Buenos Aires's current independent theatre scene. Theatre is alive in a city where there is only slight state support of the arts, where increasingly almost all artistic production is self-managed *autogestión*, and where artists are determined to make theatre anywhere and by any means available. In spaces like Timbre 4, the lines are blurred between public and private space, art and life, actor and spectator, as theatre becomes even more vital. These two plays are the palpable results of such vitality.

Jean Graham-Jones

NOTES

1. Timbre 4's website, www.timbre4.com/historia.php (accessed 17 June 2010). All translations from Spanish are mine.

2. Interview with Natalia Blanc, "Claudio Tolcachir: 'Me conmueve la desesperación de quien se siente solo,'" *La Nación* (Buenos Aires), 16 January 2010.

3. Publicity material for *La omisión de la familia Coleman* courtesy of Timbre 4.

4. Susana Villalba, "'Lo primero es la familia.' Entrevista con Claudio Tolcachir," *Clarín* (Buenos Aires), 11 September 2005, www.clarin.com/diario/2005/11/09/espectaculos/c-01001.htm (accessed 21 June 2010).

5. Publicity materials.

6. Elisa Legon, "*La omisión de la familia Coleman*" (performance review), *Theatre Journal* 59, no.3 (October 2007): 507.

7. Claudio Tolcachir, *La omisión de la familia Coleman* (Buenos Aires: Edición del autor, 2008), back cover.

8. Macarena Trigo, "La omisión de la familia Coleman: Una poética de lo roto," in Tolcachir, *La omisión de la familia Coleman*, 25.

9. "Veronese y Tolcachir. Los argentinos que han humanizado el teatro," *El Cultural* (Madrid), 30 October 2009, elcultural.es/articulo_imp.aspx?id=26089 (accessed 18 June 2010).

10. Alejandro Cruz, "La historia de un intento despiadadamente absurdo" (performance review), *La Nación* (Buenos Aires), 28 September 2008, www.lanacion.com.ar/nota.asp?nota_id=1054169 (accessed 14 July 2010).

THE COLEMAN FAMILY'S OMISSION

A PLAY BY CLAUDIO TOLCACHIR

(2005)

TRANSLATED BY ELISA LEGON
AND JEAN GRAHAM-JONES

La omisión de la familia Coleman. Photo by Giampaolo Samà/Timbre 4

La omisión de la familia Coleman premiered on 6 August 2005, in the Timbre 4 Theatre, Buenos Aires, Argentina. The following cast and design team were involved:

ABUELA (LEONARDA)	Ellen Wolf (after 2008, Araceli Dvoskin)
MEMÉ	Miriam Odorico
VERÓNICA	Inda Lavalle
DAMIÁN	Diego Futuros
GABI	Tamara Kiper
MARITO	Lautaro Perotti
HERNÁN	Gonzalo Ruiz
DOCTOR	Jorge Castaño

Assistant Direction:	Macarena Trigo
Executive Production:	Jonathan Zak & Maxime Seugé
Book and Direction:	Claudio Tolcachir

CHARACTERS

GRANDMOTHER

MEMÉ

VERÓNICA

DAMIÁN

GABI

MARITO

HERNÁN

DOCTOR

When I think that I have known you for more than three years and that it is only now I dare speak to you for the first time! And even now it is only by letter, and only because I must. It is awful that silence can be such a fault; it is the worst of my faults, but I have committed it. Long before I committed it against you, I committed it against myself. Once silence has established itself in a house, it is hard to get it out; the more important a matter is, the more it seems one wants to keep it silent. It is almost like something frozen, increasingly hard and massive: life goes on under it, but imperceptibly.

—Marguerite Yourcenar, *Alexis* (translated by Walter Kaiser)

ACT ONE

MARITO *and* MEMÉ *are sitting on the sofa, staring forward, waiting for something to happen. The sound of the front door is heard. It is* DAMIÁN. MARITO *takes a sofa cushion and when* DAMIÁN *enters, he hits him with it several times.* DAMIÁN *exits, goes to the bathroom.* MARITO *follows him.*

MARITO: Dami! Dami! Dami!

He cannot get into the bathroom and rejoins MEMÉ.

MEMÉ: Did you sleep last night?

MARITO: Yes. Why do you ask?

MEMÉ: I didn't.

MARITO: I'm hungry.

MEMÉ: Were you restless?

MARITO: Me? Why? No.

MEMÉ: You got up, you lay back down, you got up…

MARITO: No, no, no, not me.

MEMÉ: Is it okay to do that when Memé's sleeping? It isn't, is it?

MARITO: I'm hungry.

MEMÉ: Smart-ass! Me too. Can you put the kettle on for something to
    drink?

MARITO: No.

MEMÉ: For some breakfast.

MARITO: No.

MEMÉ: Do I always have to do everything myself?

DAMIÁN *comes out of the bathroom.*

MARITO: Go into the kitchen. Damián and I need to have a conversation.

MEMÉ: I'm not going anywhere until your brother gets over it. (DAMIÁN
    enters and sits at the table.) Come on, you go.

MARITO: No, it is impossible for me, Memé.

MEMÉ: Fine: if nobody goes, nobody eats. We'll die of starvation here.

MARITO: Precisely.

DAMIÁN: Shut up, Memé.

MEMÉ: We'll die and they'll find our bones, scattered all over the sofas.

MARITO: Not mine.

MEMÉ: Sure, you too. Your bare little bones inside those pajamas, my starving bones without breakfast, and Dami's bones, stained because of all his…

DAMIÁN *gives* MEMÉ *a look, and she stops talking.*

MARITO: Damián's body will decompose faster because of his drinking; yours won't take much work because there's barely any flesh. Mine won't. Mine will take longer because I'm younger than Grandma, and because of my bodily functions.

MEMÉ: Oh, the way you talk is horrible! I'm not listening.

MARITO: Grandma will be a matter of hours.

MEMÉ: Gross, Marito! Can you imagine? Grandma decomposing on the sofa, rotting away, reeking… Just go make breakfast.

MARITO: Why?

MEMÉ: Just go make breakfast.

MARITO: Why me?

MEMÉ: Because I say so.

MARITO: Oh. Gabi doesn't have much flesh either, she won't take long.

MEMÉ: Do you know what there was in the kitchen? A half-rotten dead mouse. Why don't you go check it out?

MARITO: I already found it. Dami and I embalmed it. Now it's resting in the second drawer of your nightstand.

MEMÉ: Dami?

MARITO: Yes, Dami and I embalmed it. Check out your nightstand.

MEMÉ: A dead mouse, really. Rotten just like Grandma.

MARITO: Go check it out.

MEMÉ: Marito, please! Are you listening to yourself? Put the kettle on for breakfast.

MARITO (*putting his arm around her*): You don't get it. There are things going on around here that you shouldn't know about. It's for your own good, you see? Go to the kitchen. Damián and I need to talk alone. Go! Now!

DAMIÁN *stands up, grabs* MARITO *by the neck, and lifts him up.*

DAMIÁN: Mario, go to the kitchen and shut up.

MARITO *resists and they struggle.*

MEMÉ: Okay. Okay, *I'll* go! I'll go. I'll go, Damián, see how happy I'm going? Let go of your brother!

She looks as if she is about to exit.

MARITO: Check out your nightstand, Memé!

MEMÉ: Yes.

She exits, and GRANDMOTHER *enters.*

GRANDMOTHER: Mario, get out of the kitchen!

MEMÉ: It's me, Mother.

GRANDMOTHER: What are you going to make?

MEMÉ: Breakfast.

GRANDMOTHER: What? I'm about to die, and nobody told me?

MEMÉ: Yeah, yeah, since I never do anything…

GRANDMOTHER: You do too much, more than I wish you did.

She picks up the telephone, checks for a dial tone.

GRANDMOTHER: Hello?

She hangs up.

MEMÉ: Mom, where are the matches?

GRANDMOTHER: In the kitchen.

MEMÉ: I already checked in the kitchen, but they're not there. Could they be somewhere else?

GRANDMOTHER: They're in the kitchen; they're always in the kitchen. Check again.

MEMÉ: I don't want to turn the place inside out and find out later they're somewhere else.

GRANDMOTHER: I don't want to look for them either.

MEMÉ: Ah, you'll look for them and find them?

GRANDMOTHER: Sure!

MARITO *finds the matchbox on the sofa and tosses it to* DAMIÁN. DAMIÁN *acts like he's going to give it to* MEMÉ, *but* MARITO *takes it from him and hides it again.*

MEMÉ: Of course you'll find them. You're all so clever. You all grab them and put them in some secret place. Afterwards, you find them. Nobody tells me anything. And then? Then I end up looking like an idiot.

DAMIÁN (*heading for the bathroom*): Shut up, Memé.

GRANDMOTHER: Even Marito finds them afterwards.

MEMÉ: Marito, yeah, sure! If you give me the matches, I'll make breakfast.

GRANDMOTHER: We can't expect breakfast. Memé can't find the matches.

DAMIÁN *is heard throwing up in the bathroom.*

GRANDMOTHER: Damián! Damián!

DAMIÁN *sticks his head out but doesn't leave the bathroom.*

GRANDMOTHER: You slept here last night, didn't you?

DAMIÁN: No, Grandma.

GRANDMOTHER: I thought so.

MEMÉ: Dami, do you know where the matches are?

DAMIÁN *shuts the bathroom door in her face.*

GRANDMOTHER: Did you take them, Marito?

MARITO: Yes.

GRANDMOTHER: Why do you take the matches? You can't go around with matches. You know that.

MARITO: They're for burning the house down as a last resort, Grandma. We'll all fry, but you'll die first.

GRANDMOTHER: So you want to burn down the house?

MARITO: Precisely.

DAMIÁN (*entering*): That's a lie, Grandma.

GRANDMOTHER: And what about us?

MARITO: Inside.

GRANDMOTHER: Everybody?

MARITO: Everybody.

MEMÉ (*from the kitchen*): I quit! There is no breakfast!

MARITO: We should call Verónica that day, so she can be here too, with the midgets and Baldy.

GRANDMOTHER: They're not midgets; they're normal.

MARITO: They're midgets.

GRANDMOTHER: No!

MARITO: They're midgets; that's why she doesn't bring them over.

MEMÉ (*entering*): Dami, do you happen to have a light? (DAMIÁN *looks at her but does not answer.*) You, Marito?

MARITO: We hide them away so we can laugh at your misfortunes, Memé.

MEMÉ: Okay, then I'm laughing too.

GRANDMOTHER: I'm not laughing.

MARITO: I am.

MEMÉ: Well, I can't find them! I don't know where they are!

GRANDMOTHER: Let's think about where the matches could be. What do you say to that, Damián?

DAMIÁN *stands up and leaves the house.*

MEMÉ: Damián doesn't say anything. That's weird.

GRANDMOTHER: Did you check on top of the heater?

MARITO *passes the matches to* GRANDMOTHER, *and she hides them under her robe.*

MEMÉ: The heater? I don't think so. Well, I don't know if you turned it on.

GRANDMOTHER: No, it was hot.

MARITO: Is it that thing under the bed with the clothes on it?

GABI *enters, carrying a heavy bag filled with dirty laundry.*

GABI: I'm taking the laundry out. If anybody wants something washed, give it to me now.

GRANDMOTHER: I do. Wait!

Before exiting, she surreptitiously gives MARITO *the matches back.*

MEMÉ: Little match-boy, little match-boy. Will this box keep us tied up all morning long?

GRANDMOTHER (*in Pig Latin*): Ouyay avehay anyway oneymay? [You have any money?]

GABI (*in Pig Latin*): Esyay, Iway avehay eftlay omfray ethay alesay. [Yes, I have left from the sale.]

GRANDMOTHER (*in Pig Latin*): Ifway ouyay on'tday, Iway oday. [If you don't, I do.]

GABI: Quiet! (*Back to Pig Latin*) Eshay illway ealstay itway omfray ouyay. [She will steal it from you.]

GRANDMOTHER (*in Pig Latin*): I'veway otgay itway ellway iddenhay. [I've got it well hidden.] (*Back to English*) Wait, I'll get you my dirty clothes.

MARITO *and* MEMÉ *observe the conversation, not understanding the gibberish at all.* GRANDMOTHER *exits.*

MEMÉ: Gabi, what's up with the washing machine?

GABI: It's not working, Memé.

MEMÉ: Not working? Since when?

GABI: A month ago. (*In Pig Latin*) Urryhay upway, Andmagray. [Hurry up, Grandma.]

GRANDMOTHER (*offstage, in Pig Latin*): Omingcay! [Coming!]

MEMÉ: Who broke it?

GABI: Nobody broke it; it broke on its own.

MEMÉ: Thank goodness! I would've been blamed for that too.

GRANDMOTHER *enters.*

GABI: Put it here. That's it? I put Damián's stuff in already.

MEMÉ: Are you taking it now?

GABI: I just said I was taking it.

MEMÉ: Oh, I didn't hear you. Wait, I have some. I'll get it.

MEMÉ *rushes out to get her clothes.*

GRANDMOTHER: Marito, give Gabi your PJs, so she can take them.

MARITO: Now is not the time.

GRANDMOTHER: Yes, it's the time. Give her the pajamas.

MARITO: It will be impossible, Grandma.

GABI: Come on, Marito. I'm in a hurry.

MARITO: It will be impossible, Gabi.

GABI: Fine.

MARITO: Maybe my socks.

GABI: Okay, give me your socks, then.

GRANDMOTHER: He's got to take those pajamas off once and for all!

GABI: It is impossible for him now. He can at least give me his socks.

GRANDMOTHER: Goodness!

GABI: Come on, Mario. Give me your socks.

MARITO: My socks?

GABI: Yes, your socks.

MARITO: My socks?

GABI: Yes!

MARITO: No. I can't give you my socks.

GRANDMOTHER: But didn't you just tell her to take your socks?

MARITO: Yes, I said my socks.

GABI: So?

MARITO: But not my socks.

GRANDMOTHER: Mario, please!

GABI: Let's see, Mario. How long have you been wearing those?

MARITO: A few years.

GABI: Then they smell, they're dirty. We have to wash them, understand?

MARITO: Yes, you fucking bitch. I'm not an idiot.

GABI: Give them to me then, so I can go get them washed.

MARITO: Yes, but not my socks.

GABI: Sorry, Grandma! He's going to stay filthy!

GRANDMOTHER: Wait for Memé! She's getting her clothes.

GABI: I can't wait for Memé.

She leaves.

GRANDMOTHER: You're aware that you stink, aren't you?

MARITO: Yes.

GRANDMOTHER: So?

MARITO: But not my socks.

GRANDMOTHER: You know best.

MEMÉ *enters carrying a lot of clothes.*

MEMÉ: Where did Gabi go?

GRANDMOTHER: You took too long.

MEMÉ: I told her to wait for me!

GRANDMOTHER: Go after her.

MEMÉ (*leaves her clothes and exits*): Gabi!

GRANDMOTHER: But take the clothes, Memé!

MEMÉ *returns, takes her clothes, and heads for the door.*

MEMÉ: Gabi! Gabi!

GABI *has left. Annoyed,* MEMÉ *drops her clothes on the ground.*

MEMÉ: Why didn't she wait for me?

MARITO: Calm down, Memé. I didn't get anything washed either.

MEMÉ: What do I do with all the clothes I need to wash?

GRANDMOTHER: Come, come here. (*She sits* MEMÉ *on her lap.*) People can't always be waiting around for you.

MARITO: I'm hungry.

GRANDMOTHER: Breakfast, Memé!

MEMÉ: The kettle!

She exits. MARITO *tosses the matches to* GRANDMOTHER, *who hides them again under her robe.* MEMÉ *comes back.*

MEMÉ: Where are the matches?

MARITO: Maybe I have them on me…

MEMÉ: Not so. He doesn't have them, does he?

GRANDMOTHER: Are you asking me?

MEMÉ: Oh, come on! If you have them, give them to me.

MARITO: Look for them.

MEMÉ: Does he have them, Grandma?

GRANDMOTHER: I don't know. Look for them.

MARITO: Maybe, Memé, maybe Marito has them.

MEMÉ *searches* MARITO.

MEMÉ: Let's see if that darned thief Marito has them. Let's see if this cute little boy has them. Let's look around here. No, not in his little armpits. In his little bottom, maybe? No, not in his little bottom either. And his little toy?

GRANDMOTHER (*laughing*): Oh, Memé, you're so silly.

MEMÉ: If Marito doesn't have them, then who does?

MARITO: Grandma.

MEMÉ: Of course! Grandma.

GRANDMOTHER (*abrupt*): Don't even think about it. Go look for the matches and stop playing around like a moron.

MEMÉ: I'm starting to get annoyed.

GRANDMOTHER: Me too.

MARITO: Me too.

Pause. The front door is heard opening.

MARITO: The little toy.

DAMIÁN *enters.*

DAMIÁN: Memé.

He shows her a lighter. MEMÉ *grabs it and jumps on top of* DAMIÁN *to hug him. He gets away. He picks up the phone and checks for a dial tone.*

MEMÉ: I'm going to look for matches!

She exits and comes back.

MEMÉ: Oh, Mario, I checked. We're grownups. There is no dead mouse in my drawer.

She exits.

MARITO: Ah.

DAMIÁN: Grandma.

GRANDMOTHER: Marito, come with me. You can help me with some boxes I have on top of the wardrobe.

MARITO: It will be impossible, Grandma.

GRANDMOTHER: Come on! You can help me with my zipper and clean my dentures. Come on.

GRANDMOTHER *exits.* DAMIÁN *collapses on the sofa.* MARITO *doesn't manage to leave; he comes back to the sofa walking slowly, trying not to make any noise.* DAMIÁN *turns over.*

MARITO: Go on sleeping, go on sleeping.

He sits down next to DAMIÁN.

MARITO: Dami, we have to talk. We are the only ones who can do anything, Damián. Last night, Grandma coughed all night long. She had a cold all night. I think this is a clear sign that she's pregnant, Dami. I'm letting you know because there are only two men in this house, so it's either yours or mine. If it's mine, I'd like someone to let me know.

DAMIÁN: That's not true, Mario.

MARITO: Yes, it is.

DAMIÁN: No, it isn't.

MARITO: Why not?

DAMIÁN: Because.

MARITO: Damián, it is true.

DAMIÁN *takes his backpack and heads for the door, but* MARITO *does not let him leave.*

MARITO: We need to be ready just in case, you know. Grandma is old and takes pills, but she takes pills that don't work anymore. They're the same pills from five years ago, the ones Grandma takes. Pills have an expiration date. They have to be changed; they have to be replaced periodically... Vote, vote.

DAMIÁN: What?

MARITO: Vote, Damián, vote.

DAMIÁN: Vote for what?

MARITO: Grandma needs new pills; they have to be changed. Vote!

DAMIÁN *starts to laugh.* MARITO *exits.* GABI *enters.*

GABI: Coast clear?

DAMIÁN: For the time being.

GABI: Sure, never completely.

DAMIÁN: For now.

GABI: For now? For a few hours.

DAMIÁN *gestures for her to sit down on the sofa next to him. He makes a tender yet brusque gesture, to which she responds roughly as well.*

DAMIÁN: Can I ask you a question?

GABI: No. (*Pause.*) Fine.

DAMIÁN: Who's it going to be?

GABI: What?

DAMIÁN: Who's going to leave?

GABI: Who's going to leave? Of all of us?

DAMIÁN: Okay, of all of us. Who?

GABI: You, obviously.

DAMIÁN: I don't know.

GABI: I don't have enough.

DAMIÁN: There will never be enough.

GABI: I know.

DAMIÁN: I don't either.

GABI: What?

DAMIÁN: I don't have enough.

GABI: No, not you.

DAMIÁN: It's true. Me neither.

GABI: But then, who?

MEMÉ *enters.*

MEMÉ: Gabi, you left and I couldn't give you my laundry.

GABI: Well, it's done. I was in a hurry, Memé.

MEMÉ: Yes, I see. What are you doing now?

GABI: What does it matter to you?

MEMÉ: Fine! I'm not going to copy what you do.

GABI: Copy what?

MEMÉ: I want to make clothes too.

GABI: Really? Don't touch my machine.

MEMÉ: And how do I do it without a machine?

DAMIÁN: Mom.

MEMÉ: I'm going. I don't want to be a bother in my own home. I'm going.

MEMÉ *exits.*

GABI: So, Memé.

They laugh.

GABI: So?

DAMIÁN: And you?

GABI: What?

DAMIÁN: Is there anybody?

GABI: Nobody.

DAMIÁN: Do you want...?

GABI: No.

DAMIÁN: Never again?

GABI: I hope not.

MEMÉ *enters, looking for something.*

GABI: Memé! How about you? Anyone? (*Silence.*) No changes there. (*Silence.*) Did she leave?

DAMIÁN: Yes.

GABI: Scary.

DAMIÁN: Idiot.

MARITO *enters.*

DAMIÁN: Me too.

GABI: What?

DAMIÁN: Scary.

MARITO: Gabi, Gabi, I've got hiccups.

GABI: What's going on?

MARITO: I've got the hiccups.

GABI: I'm busy right now.

MARITO: But I don't feel good.

GABI: Go tell Grandma. I have all this sewing to do.

MARITO: Unfortunately, Grandma is dead. She's not going to be able to help me anymore.

DAMIÁN *exits.* MEMÉ *enters with the kettle and* mate. *She sits on the sofa.*

GABI: Mario, that's not true. Memé, can you take care of Marito's hiccups?

MEMÉ: No, I have to gather up all the clothes you didn't take.

GABI: Memé, it's not a game. Take care of your son.

MARITO: Make yourself useful, Memé.

MEMÉ: Nobody pays any attention to me until they need me. Then, it's "Memé this" and "Memé that." Do you have some money I can borrow, Mario?

MARITO: I have hiccups.

GABI: Fine, wait, Mario. Let me finish this and I'll help you.

MARITO: Not a problem. I'll concentrate on my breathing and measure out the little amount of air coming in. Hypothetically speaking, if I were dead and we had to embalm me, you, or Dami... No, no, I take it back: Dami, he's the oldest, he'd need to use CPR to fill my lungs with air. So, when they injected the preservative, the thorax would be erect, you know? So that when rigor mortis set in, my body would be erect, even though it'd be lying down.

MEMÉ: That's gross, Marito! Are you listening to yourself?

She goes to the patio door. GABI *gets some water to calm him down.*

MARITO: Dami, would you perform mouth-to-mouth respiration on me in case of emergency?

MEMÉ: Mommy will do it for you. Come here.

MARITO: Don't let her, Gabi.

MEMÉ: Leave your sister alone; she's busy. Come have breakfast with Mommy.

GABI: Sit down, Mario.

MEMÉ: You want us to practice, Gabi?

GABI: Sit down.

MARITO: Dami, let's practice mouth-to-mouth respiration with Gabi. So if it's necessary to embalm me, we're all trained.

MEMÉ: Mommy will do it to you now.

MARITO: Gabi, don't let her. Memé's going to fall apart.

GABI: Come, sit here, Mario.

MEMÉ: You think I'm a weakling, but all of you came out of here.

MARITO: Including Verónica.

MEMÉ: Verónica first.

MARITO: Including Gabi.

MEMÉ: Including everybody, Mario.

GABI: Take twenty sips.

MARITO: Gabi had to share with Dami. That's why they're both so tiny.

MEMÉ: Yes, of course. Because they were together in my belly. That's the drawback.

MARITO: But they had company.

MEMÉ: That's the advantage. Anyway, the mother's always there.

MARITO: What for?

MEMÉ *does not answer*.

MARITO: We should bury them together, close the circle.

MEMÉ: It's not that big a deal.

MARITO: They're connected forever. One of them has a thought and the other one knows it.

MEMÉ: I'm not so sure about that.

MARITO: Something bad happens to one, and the other cries.

MEMÉ: Now Marito's making things up.

MARITO: I'm certain of it.

MEMÉ: Yeah? How come?

MARITO: It's scientifically proven, Memé.

MEMÉ: Look how my little boy makes things up.

MARITO: It's true.

MEMÉ: Fibber!

MARITO: It's true!

MEMÉ: It's a lie!

MARITO: It's true.

MEMÉ: Yeah? How so? Let's see; come on.

MARITO *takes a bottle of water from the table and throws it at* GABI.

GABI: Ouch! You're insane!

MARITO: Dami, did you get scared?

GABI: Are you insane? Why did you try to hit me like that?

MARITO: Did you get scared, Dami?

DAMIÁN *enters hurriedly.*

DAMIÁN: What happened?

GABI: He threw a bottle at my head!

MEMÉ: Nothing happened…

GABI: You, shut up!

DAMIÁN: What the hell are you doing? Did he hurt you, Gabi?

GABI: No. Enough! Knock it off, Dami! Stop, cut it out!

DAMIÁN *and* MARITO *chase each other and fight. They exit.* GABI *tries to stop them until they end up on the street.*

MEMÉ: Gabi, don't you have some spare change? I ended up without even a buck this week.

GABI: What do you want it for?

MEMÉ: I need to buy a few things.

GABI: What did you spend your allowance on, Memé?

MEMÉ: I had to buy shampoo.

GABI: There's an entire bottle in the bathroom.

MEMÉ: Yes, but that one's terrible. It makes my hair feel like straw.

GABI: It's the one we all use, Memé.

MEMÉ: I know, but it makes my hair feel like straw.

Since GABI *does not pay her much attention,* MEMÉ *walks to the clothes and takes one of the shirts.*

MEMÉ: Oh, this one's so pretty! You added the blue trim to it.

GABI: What do you need?

MEMÉ: Pads.

GABI: We have pads. Verónica brought them the other day. They're in the bathroom.

MEMÉ: But those don't have wings.

MARITO *and* DAMIÁN *come back, still fighting.* GRANDMOTHER *enters.*

GRANDMOTHER: Gabi, your brothers are fighting!

GABI: I saw them, Grandma!

GRANDMOTHER: What happened?

MEMÉ: Nothing. Marito wanted to test whether each of them feels what happens to the other, since they're twins. So he grabbed a bottle of water and threw it at Gabi, but just to scare her.

GRANDMOTHER: That boy is so original!

GABI: Grandma!

GRANDMOTHER: Memé, bring me the stick!

MEMÉ: Marito, I'm going to go get Grandma's stick!

MARITO *and* DAMIÁN *continue to fight on the floor.* MEMÉ *enters with a large stick and gives it to* GRANDMOTHER.

GRANDMOTHER: Mario, get in the shower!

MEMÉ: Damián started it.

GRANDMOTHER: Give me the stick, Memé!

MEMÉ: Marito, Grandma's coming with the stick, and she's going to beat the shit out of you both!

MEMÉ *grabs a cushion and jumps on the boys to join in the fight.* GRANDMOTHER *and* GABI *try to separate them.*

GRANDMOTHER: Get out, Memé. Don't be an idiot. Stop it! Go take a shower, Marito. Damián, what did I say?

DAMIÁN *goes into the bathroom banging the door.* MARITO *jumps on* GABI's *clothes, and tosses them in the air.*

GABI: No, Mario, no!

GABI *remains motionless. The scene freezes.* MARITO *sits at the table, ignoring what he has just done.* GABI *takes her bicycle and leaves the house banging the door.*

MEMÉ: This house is hell, isn't it?

GRANDMOTHER: Go take a shower.

MEMÉ: Okay, Mom, enough. It's over.

GRANDMOTHER: To the shower. Now!

MEMÉ: Now, Mario, to the shower. Come on.

MARITO: Now?

MEMÉ: Yes, now.

MARITO: No, now is impossible.

MEMÉ: He doesn't want to take a shower now.

GRANDMOTHER: Mario, to the shower.

MARITO: It's not convenient for me to bathe now.

MEMÉ: Do it for your granny.

MARITO: I don't recommend bathing now.

GRANDMOTHER: It'll do your head some good. Take him, Memé!

MEMÉ: Come on, let's take a shower. No whining.

MARITO: My hair will get wet.

GRANDMOTHER: Even better, you can get rid of those curls you don't like.

MEMÉ: Of course, water gets rid of curls.

MARITO: But they come back later. That's why we should straighten it, Grandma.

GRANDMOTHER: You take a shower and afterwards I'll straighten your mop.

MARITO and MEMÉ *walk toward the bathroom.*

MARITO: I disagree.

MEMÉ: Don't you want me to put shampoo on your big old head?

MARITO: You have to unplug the iron.

GRANDMOTHER: Of course, unplugged.

MARITO: Turn on the iron, Grandma.

GRANDMOTHER: Yes, yes.

They go in the bathroom. DAMIÁN *returns and starts tidying up the room.*

MARITO: But I'm not going to take off my clothes.

MEMÉ: Marito! What do you mean you are going to take a shower with your clothes on?

Water from the shower is heard.

MARITO: Well, the water's cold.

MEMÉ: Yes, it comes out cold.

GRANDMOTHER: It'll get hot.

MEMÉ: Okay, take off your clothes, Mario.

MARITO: No.

MEMÉ: You're going to take a shower with your clothes on?

MARITO: Yes, that's the condition.

MEMÉ (*appears*): He doesn't want to take his clothes off.

GRANDMOTHER: Take your clothes off, Marito! How are you going to shower with your clothes on?

MARITO (*appears*): That's the condition: the clothes don't come off.

MEMÉ: What do I do? Do I bathe him with his clothes on?

GRANDMOTHER: How are you going to bathe him with his clothes on, Memé? What are you talking about?

MEMÉ: Well… If he doesn't want to take them off… What do you want me to do? To force him?

MARITO: It's warming up.

GRANDMOTHER: Do I have to come myself?

MEMÉ: You come.

DAMIÁN *goes into the bathroom and gets fully-clothed* MARITO *under the shower.*

DAMIÁN: Knock it off, Mario. Just take the shower.

MEMÉ: You wanted to shower with your clothes on; go ahead and shower with your clothes on. Do you want shampoo?

DAMIÁN *comes back to the living room.*

MARITO (*appearing at the living room window, to* DAMIÁN): The sneakers couldn't get wet.

MEMÉ: A warm shower for Marito; Marito and Memé.

Both go into the bathroom.

GRANDMOTHER: Come, Damián, come on. Come here.

She takes him by the arms and sits him on her lap.

GRANDMOTHER: You've had enough, right?

DAMIÁN: For now.

GRANDMOTHER: No, you've had enough. You want to leave.

DAMIÁN: No, Grandma. What are you talking about?

GRANDMOTHER: You need to leave. It makes sense. But don't get so angry. Otherwise, you won't want to see us anymore, and that wouldn't be right. Don't be so angry. We're your family; that's how things are. What are you going to do?

MARITO (*appears with a towel around his waist*): Grandma, the iron.

GRANDMOTHER: Yes, yes.

MARITO *stands outside.*

DAMIÁN: Do you have money?

GRANDMOTHER: Yes.

DAMIÁN: Good. (*He stands up and takes a watch from his pant pocket.*) Take it.

GRANDMOTHER: Ah. Should we leave it in the little drawer, just in case?

DAMIÁN: No. It's for you to wear.

GRANDMOTHER: Don't you need it anymore?

DAMIÁN: For now…

GRANDMOTHER: Okay, thanks.

MEMÉ (*from the bathroom*): Mom, I can't turn the faucets off.

GRANDMOTHER: Turn them off! What do you mean you can't turn the faucets off?

MEMÉ: I don't know, they're old. They must be broken.

GRANDMOTHER: How can a faucet break?

MEMÉ: What do I know! Who knows how old they are…

GRANDMOTHER: You can't even turn a faucet off, Memé!

MEMÉ: They're old. They must be broken. We might need to replace them.

GRANDMOTHER: When you get paid, go buy some faucets and we'll replace them.

MARITO *enters wearing the towel and picks up the phone.*

Marito: Hello? There is a call!

DAMIÁN *takes the phone from him.*

DAMIÁN (*interested*): Hello. (*Curt.*) Oh, hello. Yes. No, she's out. What do you care?

MARITO: Who is it, Dami?

MEMÉ: Who is it?

GRANDMOTHER: Who is it?

DAMIÁN: It's Verónica, Mario.

MEMÉ (*entering*): Oh, Vero! I want to talk to her!

DAMIÁN: Take it, Grandma. It's Verónica.

DAMIÁN *hands the phone over to* GRANDMOTHER *and goes to the bathroom to turn the faucets off.*

GRANDMOTHER: Verónica. How are you? Yes, I am at home. I'm not going out.

MEMÉ: Can I speak to her?

GABI *enters with the bicycle.*

MARITO: Gabi, there's a call!

GABI: Who is it?

MARITO: Verónica. She says get ready for the funeral because the midgets died.

GABI: What happened?

MARITO: Baldy ran over them when he was taking the car out of the garage.

GABI: What? Grandma, give me the phone.

She takes it from her.

GABI: Hi, Vero. What happened? No, Mario said something about the kids. You're right. Listen to me…

GABI *exits with the phone.*

MEMÉ: Don't hang up, Gabi!

GRANDMOTHER: Verónica's coming over.

MARITO: With the kids?

GRANDMOTHER: No, by herself. Memé, go get some pastries.

MEMÉ: Hold on. I didn't talk to her yet.

GRANDMOTHER: You'll talk to her when she gets here.

MEMÉ: Gabi, can I talk to her?

GABI (*outside*): I am not hysterical. What happened is not a joke.

MARITO *sits on the sofa.*

MARITO: Go get some pastries, Memé.

MEMÉ: Wait. I want to talk to her.

GABI (*outside*): We don't allow him! He does whatever he wants here.

MARITO: I'm hungry.

MEMÉ: Let me talk to her afterwards, Gabi!

GABI: Okay, if you're coming over, we'll talk about it. Okay, wait, I'll put her on.

MEMÉ: Is she coming over now?

GRANDMOTHER: That's what I told you.

GABI: Grandma, she wants to talk to you.

GABI *gives* GRANDMOTHER *the phone.*

MEMÉ: Grandma already talked to her, Gabi!

GRANDMOTHER (*on the phone*): No, they just fought like a couple of brothers, that's all.

GABI (*walks over to* MARITO): Mario, what you did wasn't right. You will never do it again. Is that clear?

MARITO *looks at her and kisses her hand.*

GRANDMOTHER (*on the phone*): If you want, I'll put him on. Marito, Verónica wants to talk to you.

She gives MARITO *the phone.* MEMÉ *tries to grab it.*

MARITO: Hi, Verónica? Look, I can't talk to you right now because we're waiting for the phone to ring.

GRANDMOTHER: Memé, go get the pastries.

MEMÉ: I didn't talk yet!

GRANDMOTHER: You'll talk later.

MARITO: So will you bury them together? You know, since they're midgets, you can fit them both into the same coffin.

GABI *runs to* MARITO *and takes the phone from him.*

GABI: What on earth…? Hello, Vero? She hung up. She wasn't talking.

MEMÉ: But I didn't talk.

GABI: Verónica is coming over now; you'll talk to her then.

MARITO: No. Verónica says she isn't coming.

GRANDMOTHER: Go get some pastries.

MARITO: Verónica's not coming.

GRANDMOTHER: She *is* coming. Go, take this. Here's your chance to buy what you need. Make the most of it.

MEMÉ *approaches, takes the money* GRANDMOTHER *gives her, and runs out of the house.*

MARITO: The two hydrocephalic midgets passed away.

GABI (*to* GRANDMOTHER): You do realize that this can't go on, right?

GRANDMOTHER: We should (*in Pig Latin*) avehay imhay ommittedcay [have him committed].

GABI: Who?

GRANDMOTHER: Everybody. Well, let's make the house look pretty because Verónica's coming over.

GABI: Yes, let's make the house look pretty because Verónica's coming over.

GRANDMOTHER (*to* MARITO): What are you looking at?

MARITO: The iron.

GRANDMOTHER: Not today. It's too hot.

MARITO: It makes no difference.

GRANDMOTHER: Yes, it does make a difference. Once, I had it done in summer. It was ninety degrees out. You remember, Gabi? I ended up with my hair completely brown and in ringlets.

MARITO: No, not ringlets.

GRANDMOTHER: Yes, ringlets, all in a row.

MARITO: No, not ringlets.

GRANDMOTHER: I'll show you; I have photos.

MARITO: No, I won't look at them.

GRANDMOTHER: Yes. I'll show them to you. I'll show you all the pictures, one by one.

She exits.

MARITO: Not ringlets. It's impossible.

GABI *takes one of the dresses and sits down at the table to mend it.*

MARITO: Are you sad because of Verónica's little kids?

GABI: I am not talking to you.

MARITO: Baldy ran over the hydrocephalic midgets.

GABI: They're not midgets and nobody ran over them.

MARITO: It's a shame they've gone away forever.

GABI: Well, yeah.

MARITO: Because they were cute little blonds.

GABI: What's that got to do with it?

MARITO: Haven't you noticed there are no blonds in the family? We're a family of brunettes.

GABI: That's true.

MARITO: No.

GABI: No?

MARITO: You're forgetting Grandma. Grandma's blond.

GABI: But who knows what color Grandma's hair was before.

MARITO: Are you saying she wasn't a blond?

GABI: I don't think so.

MARITO: Then you're right, Gabi. All brunettes.

GABI: Memé's more of a light brown.

MARITO: No, Memé's a brunette.

GABI: Memé's light brown.

MARITO: Memé's a brunette, Gabi. End of debate. You and Damián have the same hair.

GABI: More or less.

MARITO: The same. Because you have the same father, Gabi, who apparently had hair like yours, brunette. Because it's not like Memé's. Memé's more of a light brown, you know? And you two are brunettes. You can tell that you're like that because of your father, who must have brown hair.

GABI: Well, you and Verónica have the same father, and your hair's not the same.

MARITO: No. Verónica has wavy hair but no ringlets.

GABI: And you have the same father.

MARITO: But don't you know why that is?

GABI: Why?

MARITO: Because Verónica didn't live here, and I do.

GABI: Oh.

MARITO: Water either makes your hair curly or it doesn't: that changes everything.

GABI: Maybe that's why, huh.

MARITO: If he'd taken me, I would have wavy hair somewhere else, and Verónica's would be straight here.

GABI: Would you have liked that?

MARITO: What?

GABI: To have been taken to live in another house.

MARITO: No.

GABI: Are you sure?

MARITO: Yes.

GABI: Well, all the better, then.

Pause.

MARITO: Gabi.

GABI: What?

MARITO: What's strange is why…

GABI: Why what?

MARITO: Why did they take her and not me?

GABI: I don't know, Mario.

GRANDMOTHER *enters.*

GRANDMOTHER: Gabi, go see why Memé's not back yet.

MEMÉ *enters with the pastries.* MARITO *exits.*

GABI: Here's Memé.

GRANDMOTHER: Give me the pastries. Gabi, bring a plate and put the kettle on for the *mate.*

GABI: What are we going to have, *mate* or tea?

MEMÉ: Why don't we make some coffee?

GABI: There's no coffee, Memé.

GRANDMOTHER: What does she usually drink?

GABI: She doesn't drink anything; she brings a bottle of water and barely lets it rest on the table.

GRANDMOTHER: Enough, Gabi.

MEMÉ: But couldn't we have coffee today?

GABI: I'm making *mate,* since she won't drink anything, anyway.

GABI *exits.* MEMÉ *shows* GRANDMOTHER *a new lipstick.*

MEMÉ: Take a look at that color!

GRANDMOTHER: Hand it to me.

MEMÉ: I'll put some on you.

GRANDMOTHER: Careful, Memé.

MEMÉ (*starts putting makeup on* GRANDMOTHER): I'm good at putting on your makeup. Say "oh." That's not "oh"; that's "ee." You know, the other day I was talking with Vero and she asked me if I'd watch the kids.

GRANDMOTHER: When did you talk to her?

MEMÉ: Wednesday.

GABI *enters with pastries and* mate.

GABI: What are you doing?

GRANDMOTHER: You didn't tell me.

MEMÉ: I was telling Mom that I talked to Verónica the other day and she asked me if I'd watch the kids. Baldy's going on a trip and she has to organize an event.

GABI: She asked you to watch her kids?

MEMÉ: She implied as much the other day. I'm letting you know so you can get organized, because I'll be gone for a few days.

GABI: We'll get by, Memé. Don't worry. It sounds strange, though.

GRANDMOTHER: Yes.

MEMÉ: Why? She invited me.

GRANDMOTHER: Why didn't you tell me?

MEMÉ: It slipped my mind. Besides, it was between Verónica and me. I don't have to tell you everything.

GRANDMOTHER: So many things are happening to you lately...

MEMÉ: More than you know.

GRANDMOTHER: I imagine.

MEMÉ: Mind your own business.

GRANDMOTHER: So long as you don't bring home another little present.

MEMÉ: Grandma, don't be crude!

GRANDMOTHER: Do I look pretty?

GABI: No. What did you do to yourself?

GRANDMOTHER: Memé put some makeup on me.

GABI: Her mouth is a mess.

MEMÉ: Her mouth looks great.

GABI: She looks like a clown.

GABI *fixes the makeup on* GRANDMOTHER's *mouth.*

MEMÉ: And so what if I have another little present? I haven't ruled out having another child.

GABI: Shut up, Mom.

GRANDMOTHER: Don't count on me. I've done my share.

GABI: Seriously, Mom? You'd have another child? What for?

MEMÉ: I don't know. I was very young when I gave birth to you all. Sometimes I feel I wasn't a very good mother. I didn't want to have you; you just happened.

GRANDMOTHER: Shut up, Memé!

GABI: And now you feel like it?

MEMÉ: Now it's like I'm ready to have a baby.

GRANDMOTHER: My hair, Gabi?

GABI *fixes* GRANDMOTHER's *hair.*

MEMÉ: Not on my own. With a partner, a husband. After all, I never got married.

GRANDMOTHER: Memé getting married in a church. That I'd like to see!

MEMÉ: Don't think I am going to stay in this house forever!

GABI: Mom, why didn't you ever live with Verónica's dad?

MEMÉ: I did.

GRANDMOTHER: The water's going to boil, Gabi.

GABI: What do you mean, you did?

GRANDMOTHER: What are you saying, Memé?

MEMÉ: Yes, we lived together for a few weeks.

GRANDMOTHER: A week. Are you done with Memé's retrospective?

GABI: A week? And then?

MEMÉ: Living together again didn't come up.

GABI: Didn't come up?

GRANDMOTHER: Evidently, it didn't come up. Okay? Are you done with the Memé retrospective?

GABI: No. Why didn't it come up?

MEMÉ: He was very uptight.

GRANDMOTHER: He was uptight.

MEMÉ: And I was very young. I didn't know how things were, and he didn't have any patience.

GRANDMOTHER: Gabi, the kettle.

GABI: What's wrong, Grandma? Can't I talk with Memé?

GRANDMOTHER: Some things are better off not remembering.

MEMÉ: Then I got pregnant and all hell broke loose.

GRANDMOTHER: Men!

MEMÉ: What?

GRANDMOTHER: We never had any luck with them.

MEMÉ: Well, I still have time. And how about you, Gabi?

GABI: What?

GRANDMOTHER: You do have time to try again.

GABI: I don't want to try again.

GRANDMOTHER: But you're so young…

GABI: I don't want to talk about it, Grandma. You know that.

GRANDMOTHER: There are some nice, smart boys around here.

GABI: Don't even think of introducing me to anybody.

MEMÉ: And if we go to a dance together?

GABI: I don't want to go to a dance. I don't want to meet anyone. I don't want anything. Okay?

MEMÉ: Come on, Gabi. You could do it for me.

GABI: And my dad?

MEMÉ: What about him?

GABI: Isn't there any way of finding out where he is?

Brief pause. MEMÉ *looks at* GRANDMOTHER. VERÓNICA *enters.* MEMÉ *jumps up from the sofa to greet her.*

VERÓNICA: Hi, what's going on? Isn't the doorbell working?

MEMÉ: Hi, Vero. You took your time.

VERÓNICA: We spoke five minutes ago, Mom.

MEMÉ: No, I didn't speak. They refused to give me the phone. I don't know why.

VERÓNICA: Never mind. Hi, Gabi. Hi, Grandma. This is a quick visit. I have a car outside waiting for me.

MEMÉ: Aren't you staying for dinner?

GABI: It's eleven in the morning, Mom.

MEMÉ: It was a joke, Gabi!

VERÓNICA: No, everything ended up getting complicated, and I don't have anyone to pick up the kids. How are you, Grandma?

GRANDMOTHER: Just fine. And yourself?

VERÓNICA: Fine, fortunately.

MEMÉ: Come, sit down. Gabi, bring…

GABI: What?

MEMÉ: Bring something for your sister. What will you have, Vero? *Mate,* coffee, tea, smoothie?

VERÓNICA: No, I just dropped by. I brought my water with me.

GABI: Well, I'll bring some *mate.*

GABI *exits.* MARITO *enters, holding a bottle.*

MEMÉ: That's right. Bring the *mate.* Of course she will have some.

VERÓNICA: How are you, Marito?

MARITO: Didn't the kids come?

VERÓNICA: No, they're at school. I have to go pick them up now.

MARITO: Don't they take the school bus?

VERÓNICA: Sometimes.

MARITO: They take the school bus.

VERÓNICA: How do you know my children take the bus?

MARITO: Do they or don't they?

VERÓNICA: Sometimes.

MARITO: They do.

VERÓNICA: I am asking you: how do you know my children take the bus?

MEMÉ: Gabi, get your sister a glass!

VERÓNICA: No need, Memé. Really. What are you drinking, Mario?

MEMÉ: You'll drink from a glass. It's no bother.

VERÓNICA: I'm used to it. I take my bottle of water everywhere.

MEMÉ: Gabi!

VERÓNICA: Please! (*She stands up.*) Dami, I didn't see you there. How are you?

DAMIÁN *ignores her.*

MEMÉ: Ask him what state he was in when he got home this morning.

VERÓNICA: You look so pretty, Grandma. You're all dolled up.

GRANDMOTHER: I wasn't so dolled down that I needed to doll up either.

VERÓNICA: Oh, Grandma!

MEMÉ: Mom, be quiet! So you drink a lot of water?

VERÓNICA: Yes, more or less.

MEMÉ: How much?

VERÓNICA: I don't know; maybe eight glasses a day.

MEMÉ: Eight glasses!

VERÓNICA: Yes, that's what they say you should drink…

MEMÉ: Because of the diet.

VERÓNICA: Grandma, I brought you that hand lotion I had promised.

She gives GRANDMOTHER *a jar.*

GRANDMOTHER: How nice!

MEMÉ: Silly me! What could water have to do with your diet?

VERÓNICA: Try it. It's very good. If it doesn't work, I'll buy another one.

GABI *enters with the* mate.

GRANDMOTHER: What does it say here? Most…

GABI: It must be moisturizer.

VERÓNICA: Yes, a moisturizer.

MEMÉ (*takes the jar from* GRANDMOTHER *and reads*): Let me see. Moisturizer, hand and foot lotion.

GRANDMOTHER: I needed something for my feet.

MARITO *takes the jar from her and tosses it to* DAMIÁN. DAMIÁN *catches it and throws it out the window. At first, nobody reacts.* MEMÉ *meets* VERÓNICA*'s eyes and reacts.*

MEMÉ: Guys, what's all that about? How can you throw things at each other like that? What is this, a madhouse?

GRANDMOTHER: Very good, Memé. Now you can get the lotion for me, please.

MEMÉ *exits to get the lotion and comes back, putting some on.*

VERÓNICA: Grandma, what is Mario drinking?

MARITO: Hey, Vero. Did she get better?

VERÓNICA: Who?

MARITO: Did she get better or not?

VERÓNICA: Who?

MARITO: She got better.

VERÓNICA: I don't know what you're talking about, Mario.

MEMÉ: Who got better, Mario?

MARITO: The teacher.

MEMÉ: What teacher?

VERÓNICA: How do you know that?

MARITO: She recovered. The transfusion was a success.

VERÓNICA: Mario.

GABI: What's going on?

MARITO: All the kids in Room B gave blood, Gabi.

MEMÉ: Mario, how are kids going to give blood?

MARITO: Not yours, right? They were let off because they're different.

VERÓNICA: Grandma, does anyone watch Mario to see what he does, where he goes?

GRANDMOTHER: Memé's in charge of that.

GABI: How are we supposed to watch him all day long, Verónica?

GRANDMOTHER: Don't pay any attention to this goof.

MEMÉ: He's not serious.

VERÓNICA: Yes, it's serious.

GABI: Yes, it's serious, Grandma.

MARITO: Of course it's serious. They didn't take the midgets' blood.

VERÓNICA: Mario, I don't like you talking about my children. And least of all like that. Is that clear?

MARITO: But I love them very much.

VERÓNICA: Fine, thanks, but don't.

MARITO: Don't?

VERÓNICA: Don't. Not at all. Nothing. Is that clear?

MARITO: No. And now I'm getting worked up.

VERÓNICA: All I ask is that you keep an eye on him, please.

GABI: But what's wrong with Mario?

DAMIÁN: Nothing's wrong with Mario.

VERÓNICA: What do you know?

GABI: But what's that about blood?

DAMIÁN: Gabi, we can talk about this when we're alone, don't you think?

VERÓNICA: I'm sorry, Damián, but this matter concerns me, because he's talking about my children.

GABI: And what matter doesn't concern you? He's your brother, right?

VERÓNICA: Look, Gabi, when you have children of your own, you can have an opinion about others', you know?

MEMÉ: That's true. Only when someone has children...

DAMIÁN: Shut up, Mom!

VERÓNICA: Okay. Take it easy, Damián.

DAMIÁN: What's wrong with you?

MARITO: Don't worry, Vero. They're midgets. They don't live long.

GABI: Mario, please...

VERÓNICA: That's it! I'm leaving.

HERNÁN enters the house.

HERNÁN: Excuse me. I rang the bell, but I don't think it's working.

VERÓNICA: Hernán! What are you doing?

HERNÁN: I apologize for coming in, but you said that if you took long...

VERÓNICA: Yes, no problem. We're leaving, anyway.

GRANDMOTHER: Introduce him, Vero, introduce him!

GABI: Grandma!

GABI goes over to the sewing machine.

VERÓNICA: Yes, of course... Come in. Grandma, this is Hernán. Hernán, this is my grandmother.

GRANDMOTHER: What a looker! And me, completely widowed.

HERNÁN: And me, completely single.

VERÓNICA: My...

MEMÉ: Verónica's mother.

VERÓNICA: Memé.

HERNÁN: Your mother! A pleasure.

VERÓNICA: Yes. My mother. My brothers, and my sister Gabi over there.

GRANDMOTHER: Also single.

MEMÉ: Well, for that matter, I'm also single.

HERNÁN (*to* GABI): Excuse me. Don't I know you from somewhere?

GABI: No.

HERNÁN: I must be mistaken, then.

VERÓNICA: This is Damián, my brother.

HERNÁN: What's up?

MARITO *taps* HERNÁN's *shoulder from behind.*

VERÓNICA: And Mario.

MARITO: He's a shrimp!

MEMÉ: Mario! He is proportionate!

HERNÁN: Um, cool, Mario. You're some guy.

VERÓNICA: This is Hernán. Poor thing. He drives me everywhere.

HERNÁN: The pleasure's mine, you know?

VERÓNICA: Sorry for the short stay. Terrible week.

GRANDMOTHER: But you didn't tell us anything!

VERÓNICA: I'm wasting Hernán's time, Grandma.

GRANDMOTHER: If you pay him, it shouldn't be a bother to wait for you.

HERNÁN: No, really. It's not a problem.

MEMÉ: Don't be a drag, Vero! Just a short while.

MARITO (*to* HERNÁN): Come, sit down over here.

VERÓNICA & GABI: No!

VERÓNICA: No, really. I don't want to waste your time, Hernán.

HERNÁN: It's fine, Vero. Getting out of the car feels good. I'd take some *mate*, though, if you offered it to me.

MEMÉ: I'm just about to pour.

MARITO (*offers him the* mate): Here.

MEMÉ: I was pouring it!

MARITO (*to* MEMÉ): Get out of here!

MARITO *shoves her curtly.*

VERÓNICA: Grandma!

GRANDMOTHER: Let them become friends!

MARITO (*to* GRANDMOTHER): Grandma, who's he?

GRANDMOTHER: Verónica's driver.

MARITO: What's his name?

GRANDMOTHER: Hernán.

MARITO: Ah.

VERÓNICA: Gabi, so, do you have a lot of work?

GABI: Yes, all this is for a sale.

VERÓNICA: A sale?

DAMIÁN *moves closer to* MARITO *and* HERNÁN.

GABI: A garage sale.

HERNÁN: That's great! Are you organizing it?

GABI: Yes.

VERÓNICA: That's great, Gabi!

MEMÉ: We're helping her.

HERNÁN: Congratulations.

VERÓNICA: And where's the garage sale going to be?

GABI: I was thinking of here.

VERÓNICA: Here, at home? (VERÓNICA *notices her cell phone is vibrating.*) Hold on. It must be from work.

GABI: The idea is to take it somewhere else later.

VERÓNICA: Yes, I think so. Hello? Mónica, I know you were looking for me. No. Running errands. Yes. And what do you need? (GABI *does not answer.*) You, Gabi, I'm asking you. What do you need?

GABI: I thought you were on… A clientele.

VERÓNICA: How much?

GABI: I don't know… A group of people…

VERÓNICA (*on the phone*): How much? No, no. Check. Look on my desk, because I drafted it myself. Yes, I left it last night on my desk. (*Goes toward the clothes.*) And what is it? Clothes you find?

GABI: No, I buy them used and fix them up.

VERÓNICA: These two are really wild!

GABI: Do you like them?

VERÓNICA: Kind of.

GABI: Well, that's because they're for an older woman. Look at this one, Vero. Check it out.

VERÓNICA: Yes, yes, page 24. I'm telling you, I did it last night. Hold on, there are people around me…

VERÓNICA *tries to concentrate and goes out to the patio.* GABI *stays behind holding the blouse.*

MEMÉ (*to* HERNÁN): That would look fantastic on me.

GABI: I'm not talking to you. Nothing here is for you!

MEMÉ: And if I buy it? (*To* HERNÁN) I can buy it if I want to, right?

HERNÁN: So tell me, do you have clothing for men?

GABI: No.

GABI *heads back to the sewing machine.*

HERNÁN (*to* MARITO): Only for women, huh?

MARITO: Is your name Hernán?

HERNÁN: Yes.

MARITO: You're Verónica's driver.

HERNÁN: You bet.

MARITO (*to* GRANDMOTHER): See how much I know?

VERÓNICA: Okay, that's done. What were you showing me, Gabi?

GABI: Nothing. Never mind.

MARITO: Do you know the midgets?

HERNÁN: What midgets, Vero?

VERÓNICA: We're leaving, Hernán. Bye, Grandma.

HERNÁN: Good bye. A pleasure. Thanks for the *mate*.

VERÓNICA (*notices the watch while kissing* GRANDMOTHER): What's this? The watch turned up!

GRANDMOTHER: Yes, I found it in the little drawer.

VERÓNICA: Great! Grandma, do you have anything left over from last week?

GRANDMOTHER: Not much. I had to buy medicine for Mario and…

VERÓNICA: Take this. It's not much, really.

GABI: I'll let you know otherwise.

VERÓNICA: Please do, Gabi. Shall we, Hernán? Bye, Grandma.

HERNÁN: Bye, ma'am.

MEMÉ: Bye. Congratulations. (*Stopping* VERÓNICA *by the door*) Vero.

VERÓNICA: Yes. Sorry, Mom, bye. (*Kisses* MEMÉ.)

MEMÉ: I wanted to ask you something.

VERÓNICA: What?

MEMÉ: Are the kids okay?

VERÓNICA: Yes, Mom, fine.

MEMÉ: And Baldy?

HERNÁN *laughs.* MEMÉ *and* VERÓNICA *cast a quick glance at him.*

VERÓNICA: His name's Patricio, and he's just fine.

MEMÉ: We're all good here. Marito's a mess. Gabi's at a rough age.

VERÓNICA: What's going on, Memé?

MEMÉ: You've seen what living here is like.

VERÓNICA: I've got to go.

MEMÉ: Wait! I wanted to ask you. You have that big house and all that room. Couldn't I come live with you for a while? That way we'll get to know each other better.

VERÓNICA: No.

MEMÉ: We've never lived together, after all.

VERÓNICA: Let's go, Hernán.

MEMÉ: Just give me a tiny room.

GABI: Come here, Mom. Sit down.

MEMÉ: She can throw a mattress down on the floor. I won't be a bother.

VERÓNICA: Memé, I am sorry, no.

MEMÉ: I can help you with the kids. Since she's out at work all day, I can give her a hand.

VERÓNICA: Please, Memé. No, I mean it; no.

MEMÉ: Will you think about it?

VERÓNICA: No.

MEMÉ: Think about it.

VERÓNICA: Bye.

MEMÉ: I can help with your clothes!

VERÓNICA: Memé, stop it! No!

MARITO: Fucking bitch!

General reaction.

GABI: Marito, enough!

VERÓNICA: Grandma, if he treats me like this again, I won't ever set
    another foot in this house!

GABI *takes the bottle* MARITO's *been drinking from away from him.*

GRANDMOTHER (*to* VERÓNICA): Don't pay attention to him. He is not
    serious.

GABI: Liquor! This is liquor, Grandma!

VERÓNICA: I asked you ten times what he was drinking.

MARITO: Those hydrocephalics are gonna explode!

GRANDMOTHER: That's the last straw, Mario!

GABI: What's this?

MARITO: Gin.

MEMÉ: That bottle's mine!

VERÓNICA: I have to go.

GABI: Mom, you keep a bottle of gin in the house?

MEMÉ: I kept it hidden.

MARITO: Not really, Gabi.

VERÓNICA (*to* HERNÁN): Mario's got some problems. He's really hard
    to deal with…

HERNÁN: Yes, obviously.

MARITO: I think you're a little shrimp!

MARITO *pounces on* HERNÁN. *Everyone holds him back.*

HERNÁN: What's his issue with my height?

VERÓNICA: Ignore him.

MARITO: He's not right for you, Vero! You'll have more midgets!

DAMIÁN: Marito, come. Let's have a drink in the bathroom.

MARITO: Let's go, Dami!

GABI: You too, Damián?

DAMIÁN: Mind your own business.

GABI: How can you drink with him?

DAMIÁN: He's drinking a little, that's all.

MEMÉ (*joining in*): Considering your hangover last night…

GABI: You, shut up!

GRANDMOTHER, *little by little, starts to feel sick. Nobody notices it.*

GABI: I don't understand you, Damián!

MEMÉ: We can't keep anything in this house!

DAMIÁN (*to* HERNÁN): Beat it!

HERNÁN: Take it easy! Okay, okay!

DAMIÁN: Beat it! Verónica, get out of here!

VERÓNICA: Gabi, I'll call you tonight to find out how everything ended
    up. (*To* HERNÁN) Are you okay? Did he hurt you?

GABI: How can you leave like this?

VERÓNICA: What do you want me to do?

MARITO *locks himself in the bathroom with the bottle, while* DAMIÁN *and*
MEMÉ *struggle to get in.*

GABI: I don't know. Talk to him. He's your brother.

VERÓNICA: Look, Gabriela, I'd rather not get involved in these things.

GABI: So why aren't you going to get involved and I am?

VERÓNICA: Nobody's forcing you to.

GABI: Who'll deal with it otherwise?

VERÓNICA: We're leaving, Hernán, or do I have to walk home?

VERÓNICA *exits.*

DAMIÁN: Mario, open up!

GABI: Help me, Damián!

MARITO *opens the door.* DAMIÁN *goes in. They close the door and start to drink together.* MEMÉ *manages to get in and the three wrestle for the bottle.* GABI *remains outside, watching them. She closes the bathroom door.*

HERNÁN (*to* GABI): Can I help you in any way?

No reply.

HERNÁN: Okay, bye. See you.

He exits. GABI *comes back into the living room, takes the clothes out, and sits down at the sewing machine.* MEMÉ *manages to hold onto the almost-empty bottle, and comes back into the living room, wrapping it in her arms. She notices* GRANDMOTHER, *who is still.* MARITO *enters, and* MEMÉ *makes a gesture. Both stare at* GRANDMOTHER. MARITO *goes to the patio to look for* DAMIÁN, *who comes in quickly. All three stare at* GRANDMOTHER *in silence.* GABI, *with her back to them, is unaware of this.*

DAMIÁN: Gabi.

GABI *does not reply.*

DAMIÁN, MARITO & MEMÉ (*several times with different rhythms*): Gabi! Gabi! Gabi!

GABI: What's the matter?

Nobody replies. GABI *notices* GRANDMOTHER *and runs to her.*

GABI: Grandma, what's wrong? (*To* DAMIÁN) Call the doctor.

MARITO: Is she dead?

MEMÉ: No, not yet.

DAMIÁN (*about to hand the phone to* GABI): Here, Gabi.

GABI: Give me the phone.

DAMIÁN *hands the phone to* GABI.

MARITO: Come, Dami. Help me carry her.

GABI: Nobody touch her!

MEMÉ: Shouldn't we bring her around?

MARITO: I'll take care of this. Let me, Dami.

GABI: Please, it's an emergency.

MARITO *takes an atomizer from the dresser and aims it at* GRANDMOTHER.

GABI: No! That's poison, Marito!

DAMIÁN *pounces on* MARITO, *and they start to wrestle.*

MEMÉ: Kids, don't pick a fight now, not while Grandma's dying! (*To* GRANDMOTHER) It'll be fine, Mom.

GABI: Stop it, Damián! (*On the phone*) Yes, we need an ambulance.

MARITO *and* DAMIÁN *separate.*

MEMÉ: Tell them a big one so we can all go.

GABI: She's conscious, but she's not talking.

MARITO: Tell them she's… (*He gestures.*)

GABI: She's having trouble breathing.

MARITO *takes the bottle from the table.*

MEMÉ: No! Not again! There's barely any left!

MEMÉ *takes the bottle from* MARITO, *and* DAMIÁN *grabs it, drinks what's left, and tosses the bottle toward the patio.*

GABI: 232 Yapeyú.[1]

MEMÉ (*to* DAMIÁN): That's all we needed.

GABI: It's a house.

DAMIÁN: Tell them about the bell, Gabi!

GABI: Oh! The doorbell doesn't work, but we'll be waiting by the door.

MARITO (*approaching* GRANDMOTHER): Help me pick her up, Dami.

GABI: Don't touch her! (*On the phone*) Leonarda Coleman.

MEMÉ: Why don't we call Vero instead?

GABI: Let's see… What's Grandma's Social Security Number?[2]

Nobody knows.

GABI: Look for her card, Memé!

She doesn't know where it is. MEMÉ *washes her hands of the problem.*

GABI: 68 years old. Grandma's date of birth?

MEMÉ: May 12th…

GABI: May 12th, yes. What year?

Everybody does the math.

MEMÉ: 1930?

MARITO: Higher.

MEMÉ: 35?

MARITO: Higher, higher.

MEMÉ: 40?

MARITO: Lower.

DAMIÁN: 1937?

MARITO *nods.*

DAMIÁN: 1937, Gabi!

GABI (*back on the phone*): 1937. May 12th, yes. (*Pause.*) Oh, yes. That's right.

MEMÉ: May 12th?

GABI: Please, come as fast as you can. (*She hangs up.*)

They all look at each other, not knowing what to do.

MEMÉ: Happy birthday, Mom.

MARITO: Is it today?

GABI: Yes. I didn't realize.

MARITO *approaches* GRANDMOTHER *and kisses her.*

GABI: Happy birthday, Grandma. The ambulance is coming.

DAMIÁN: Happy birthday, Grandma.

MEMÉ: Happy birthday to you, happy birthday to you…!

Gradually, all except GABI *join in and sing "Happy Birthday." As the song is heard, lights dim on the space of the home and come up on the bed, what in the second act will be the space of the hospital. Without a pause and in a smooth transition, the first day of the second act begins.*

ACT TWO

DAY ONE:

Hospital. VERÓNICA *comes out of the bathroom and helps* GRANDMOTHER *lie down.*

VERÓNICA: Okay, Grandma, you have all your toiletries. You need anything and I'm not here, call the nurses and they'll come right away. The nurses' office is just next door. Anyway, don't worry, I'll give them a little something extra, so we make sure they watch you closely. Are you coming, Grandma?

GRANDMOTHER *comes out of the semi-darkness and walks toward the bed.* VERÓNICA *helps her into bed and makes sure she is comfortable.*

VERÓNICA: Anyway, they're fabulous people. They've been here for years. They're all warm and super professional.

GRANDMOTHER: And Gabi?

VERÓNICA: She took everyone home, because Marito was still in his pajamas and Memé… We agreed that it was better for me to bring you here myself so you weren't disturbed.

GRANDMOTHER: They'll come visit, won't they?

VERÓNICA: Grandma, what did the doctor say? That you had to rest, right? So, rest and don't worry about anything. Are you okay?

GRANDMOTHER: Very well, thank you.

VERÓNICA: Happy birthday. I am so sorry. I am so embarrassed.

GRANDMOTHER: It doesn't matter!

VERÓNICA: I'm so overwhelmed by everything. I forgot.

GRANDMOTHER: I didn't remember either.

VERÓNICA: I owe you a present. I'll bring it by tomorrow.

GRANDMOTHER: There's no need.

VERÓNICA: Hush, Grandma. Let's be quiet, Grandma.

The DOCTOR *enters.*

DOCTOR: Excuse me.

VERÓNICA: Eduardo! I'm sorry I called you like that.

DOCTOR: Don't worry about it.

VERÓNICA: We were so scared…

DOCTOR: Please, it's the least I can do.

VERÓNICA: Let me introduce you to my grandmother.

DOCTOR: Hello. How are you feeling?

GRANDMOTHER: Better.

VERÓNICA: She's a little weak, but her face now has some color.

GRANDMOTHER: I'd like to go home as soon as I can, doctor.

DOCTOR: Not yet. Now we need to run some tests and wait for the results.

VERÓNICA: Make the most of this, Grandma. A little peace and quiet never hurt anyone.

DOCTOR: Right. Are we treating you that badly?

VERÓNICA: She's always been like this: super restless, but…

DOCTOR: A little vacation won't hurt.

VERÓNICA: Isn't that so?

DOCTOR (*to* VERÓNICA): Well, as soon as the results are ready, I'll stop by. Are you staying?

VERÓNICA: Yes, a while longer, for sure.

GABI *enters.*

GABI: Hi. I made it as fast as I could.

VERÓNICA: Gabi, this is Eduardo. My sister Gabriela.

DOCTOR: Hello, how are you? I'm Eduardo.

GABI: Hello. How's Grandma?

DOCTOR: For the time being, she's stable. We need to run some tests to make sure that it's nothing serious.

GABI: But she's okay now?

VERÓNICA: He already told you she's stable.

GABI: What's wrong with her?

DOCTOR: It might be just her blood pressure. Let's wait for the results.

GABI: Is she conscious?

VERÓNICA: Yes, she's fine now.

GRANDMOTHER: Why can't you all let the body's owner speak for herself?

GABI: Grandma, you're awake.

GABI *hugs her.*

GRANDMOTHER: I think so.

DAMIÁN *enters.*

DAMIÁN: Gabi, can we come in or should we wait outside?

VERÓNICA: Did everyone come?

GABI: Yes, they all insisted on coming.

DOCTOR: Come in now, because visiting hours are just about over.

DAMIÁN *exits.*

VERÓNICA: What are you doing? Will you come by later, Eduardo?

DOCTOR: If I don't, I'll call you?

VERÓNICA: I'll leave my cell on.

DOCTOR: Great. Bye.

He exits. MEMÉ *enters.*

MEMÉ: Excuse me...

She remains standing by the door.

GRANDMOTHER: Hi, Memé!

MEMÉ: Damián and Marito are here.

GABI: Give me Grandma's bag.

MEMÉ: This place is huge!

GRANDMOTHER: Sit down, Memé.

GABI: I brought you your nightgown, Grandma.

VERÓNICA: I already bought her one.

GABI: Well, in case she needs a change.

MEMÉ: How are you?

GRANDMOTHER: Better, but take pity on me anyway.

MEMÉ (*laughs*): Mom!

VERÓNICA: Why don't you come in, Memé?

MEMÉ: May I?

VERÓNICA (*to* GABI): What's wrong with her?

GABI: Ignore her.

DAMIÁN *and* MARITO *enter.*

DAMIÁN: Hi, Grandma.

GRANDMOTHER: You all came. What an honor!

MARITO: When are we leaving?

MEMÉ: We're visiting Granny, Mario.

MARITO: I don't think this hospital thing is going to work.

DAMIÁN: Shut up, Mario. Sit over here.

GRANDMOTHER: Marito, you look so elegant!

GABI: He wanted to change his clothes for our visit, Grandma.

MARITO: The flowers.

GABI: No. The flowers are at home.

GRANDMOTHER: You were bringing me flowers?

MARITO: Yes.

GRANDMOTHER: What a gentleman!

MEMÉ: He thought you were dead. Yeah, some gentleman!

VERÓNICA: Look, this hospital is where they'll take the best care of her, okay? I want it clear this is where my entire family gets treated. Is that understood?

DAMIÁN: No.

VERÓNICA: They've known me for years, and I don't feel like having to explain anything that might happen in this room. That's all.

DAMIÁN: Are you okay here, Grandma?

GRANDMOTHER: If it's for a short time, yes.

GABI: Nothing's going to happen. What can happen?

VERÓNICA *looks at her.*

GABI: Nothing's going to happen, Verónica.

MEMÉ: May I go to the bathroom, or is that dangerous?

VERÓNICA: Please, Mom, I'm not talking about that.

MEMÉ: It's just to pee.

VERÓNICA: It's over there. Just don't touch anything.

MARITO: Grandma, they're already dividing your stuff up.

GRANDMOTHER: Who?

MARITO: Memé will take some stuff to the church, and Gabi will sell the rest at her garage sale.

GABI: Quiet, Marito.

MARITO: They already sold everything. Even your teeth.

DAMIÁN: How much does this cost, Verónica?

VERÓNICA: A lot.

DAMIÁN: But how much?

VERÓNICA: I don't know. Once I get the bills, I can show them to you, if you want.

MARITO: Do your kids get treated here?

VERÓNICA: Yes.

GABI: I want to contribute what I can too.

DAMIÁN: No, Gabi.

GABI: Why not?

VERÓNICA: It's not necessary.

GABI: We'll see later.

MARITO: And Baldy too?

VERÓNICA (*to* DAMIÁN): Why do you say "no" like that, with so much…

MARITO: Arrogance.

VERÓNICA: Well, yes. Arrogance.

MARITO: Baldy too, Vero?

VERÓNICA: I'm talking to you, Damián.

GABI: Because we know it's impossible to pay for something like this.

VERÓNICA: That's not what it sounded like.

MARITO: Baldy too, Vero?

DAMIÁN (*grabs him*): She said her entire family! Didn't you hear her say "my entire family"?

He lets go of him and exits.

VERÓNICA: Gabi, I beg you to…

GABI: Don't worry. Nothing's going to happen. What can happen?

MEMÉ *comes out of the bathroom.*

MEMÉ: This may be a private hospital, but the faucets don't work.

VERÓNICA: What do you mean they don't work?

GRANDMOTHER: Memé and her faucets!

GABI (*to* VERÓNICA): Never mind, I'll go. What did you do, Mom?

She goes into the bathroom.

MARITO: We came to take you back home, Grandma.

GRANDMOTHER: I'll come back home, you'll see.

VERÓNICA: What did you do, Memé?

MEMÉ: I didn't even sit down so I wouldn't break anything.

VERÓNICA: Are they broken?

GABI (*from the bathroom*): No.

MARITO: There are no sandwiches, no cake, no balloons; this doesn't look like a birthday party.

MEMÉ: Mario!

VERÓNICA: Is Mario still drunk?

MEMÉ: No. He was really restless so we gave him a couple of Grandma's drops.

VERÓNICA: What drops?

MEMÉ: Drops to make him fall asleep.

MARITO: But they didn't work because they're expired.

VERÓNICA: Gabi, what's going on?

MARITO: All of Grandma's medicine is expired.

GABI *comes out of the bathroom.*

GABI: Mom, you're fixated on faucets!

MEMÉ: Did they turn off?

GABI: Of course! Why wouldn't they?

VERÓNICA: Do you know anything about some drops for Mario?

GABI: Well… Sometimes there's no other alternative.

DAMIÁN *enters and heads straight into the bathroom.*

DAMIÁN: They said visiting hours are over. We've got to go.

GRANDMOTHER: Okay, go.

VERÓNICA: Yes, yes. Let's go, let's go. I don't want to have a problem on the first day. Are you staying, Gabi?

GABI: I can't. I thought you were going to stay.

VERÓNICA: No, I can't.

DAMIÁN *comes out of the bathroom.*

GABI: I can't either. Tomorrow, I have an order that is…

MARITO: Important.

VERÓNICA: Patricio's going out, and I don't have anybody to watch the kids.

MEMÉ: I can't stay.

GABI: Why not, Mom?

VERÓNICA: Anyway, Gabi…

MARITO: Vero, I'm staying.

VERÓNICA: Listen, can't you hold off on that order? Tell them the truth, that your grandmother's in the hospital.

GABI: I can't. It's the only one I'm getting paid for this week, Verónica.

MARITO: Dami and I will stay, Vero.

GABI: Can't you tell Patricio to cover for you tonight?

VERÓNICA: Hasn't it been enough?

DAMIÁN: I'm staying.

MEMÉ: Great! Dami's staying! Bye, Mom, see you tomorrow. I left the house open. I have to go lock up.

She exits.

GABI (*to* DAMIÁN): Can you?

MARITO: We men will stay at the hospital, Grandma.

DAMIÁN: No, you're leaving.

MARITO: Why?

DAMIÁN: Because.

MARITO: Oh.

VERÓNICA: Grandma, Damián's staying with you tonight, okay?

GRANDMOTHER: Not a problem. You can go too, Damián, if you want.

DAMIÁN: No, I'm staying, Grandma.

GRANDMOTHER: Okay, thanks.

VERÓNICA: Rest, Grandma. See you tomorrow.

VERÓNICA *exits.*

GABI: See you tomorrow, Grandma. Do you want me to bring anything from home?

GRANDMOTHER: No, but don't give away my stuff just yet.

GABI: Oh, Grandma!

MARITO: I'll stay here with Dami, Grandma.

GABI: Let's go, Marito.

MARITO: No.

GABI: Let's go home. You can come back tomorrow.

MARITO: Dami, don't leave her.

GRANDMOTHER: Go, so you can sleep in my bed.

GABI: That's right. Let's go. You can come back tomorrow.

MARITO: Okay, but hang in there, Grandma. Don't give your organs away to anybody, because I need them.

VERÓNICA *returns.* MARITO *grabs her.*

MARITO: Come on, Vero, visiting hours are over.

VERÓNICA: Okay. Go with Gabi. I'll be there soon.

GABI: Let's go, Marito.

They exit.

VERÓNICA: Just a minute, Damián. Careful what you do. Is that clear?

DAMIÁN: Bye, Verónica.

VERÓNICA: You know what I'm talking about, right?

DAMIÁN: I said "bye."

VERÓNICA: See you tomorrow, Grandma!

She exits.

GRANDMOTHER: Come lie down with me.

DAMIÁN: Weird birthday, huh?

GRANDMOTHER: Really.

DAMIÁN: Don't you want anything?

GRANDMOTHER: No, there is no need. Did you bring my radio?

DAMIÁN: No. What do you want? A radio?

GRANDMOTHER: There isn't one here. Tomorrow they'll bring me mine.

DAMIÁN: No, you wait here. I'll be right back.

DAMIÁN *exits, and at the same time,* GABI *and* MEMÉ *enter with a bag, followed by* MARITO, *whose hand is bandaged. He tosses a bloodstained handkerchief on the floor. The second day begins.*

DAY TWO:

GABI: Memé, put Grandma's things in the closet. Hi, Grandma, how are
    you feeling?

GRANDMOTHER: So-so.

MEMÉ: I don't think they'll fit.

She goes into the bathroom.

GABI: Store whatever you can. It's not that much, anyway. (*To*
    GRANDMOTHER) What? Are you dizzy?

MEMÉ (*in the bathroom*): Should I stack things or hang them up?

GABI: Figure it out, Memé! Did the doctor see you today?

GRANDMOTHER: Yes, but they said he'd be back later.

MEMÉ (*entering*): It's better if the nurses hang things up.

MARITO: I'm bleeding, Gabi.

GABI: I brought your slippers, Grandma.

GRANDMOTHER: Thank you.

MARITO: It won't stop bleeding, Gabi.

GABI: Mario, enough!

GRANDMOTHER: What happened?

MARITO: Memé with a knife, last night.

GRANDMOTHER: What? What happened?

GABI: Nothing, Grandma.

MEMÉ: It was an accident. You started playing with the knife!

MARITO: The cut won't close up.

VERÓNICA: Hi. Sorry I was running late, but…

GABI: The doctor hasn't shown up yet.

VERÓNICA *sees the bloodstained handkerchief on the floor.*

VERÓNICA: What's that bloody handkerchief doing on the floor?

MARITO: Marito, bleeding to death.

GABI: Marito, put a band-aid on or something. Please, Memé.

MEMÉ: I can't stand the sight of blood, Gabi.

VERÓNICA: Can you go wash up, Marito? The doctor will be here any
     minute. Give me a mop, Memé.

MEMÉ: Where am I going to get one? Let's ask the nurses!

VERÓNICA: No, just leave it.

VERÓNICA *picks up the handkerchief and takes it to the bathroom.*

VERÓNICA: Grandma, how are you?

GRANDMOTHER: So-so.

MEMÉ: Vero, why don't you take Marito to the ER? Maybe he needs
     stitches or something.

MARITO: No, he doesn't need any stitches.

GABI: Will they be able to see him, Verónica?

VERÓNICA (*coming back in*): Yeah… I don't know.

DAMIÁN *enters.*

VERÓNICA: Dami, can you take him to the Emergency Room? It looks like he's wounded.

DAMIÁN: How did you do it?

MARITO: Grandma's nurse bit me.

MEMÉ: That's a lie! I did it to him last night with a knife.

DAMIÁN: Why?

MEMÉ: It was an accident.

MARITO: It wasn't an accident. This wasn't an accident.

MEMÉ: Are you accusing me?

MARITO: Stuff's been happening at home since you left, Grandma.

VERÓNICA: Damián, give me your backpack.

DAMIÁN: What is wrong with you?

VERÓNICA Give me your backpack. Don't play dumb. Give me your backpack right now.

GABI: Verónica.

DAMIÁN: Shut up.

VERÓNICA: Not here, you understand? They'll check you on the way out; they always check. Don't be stupid.

DAMIÁN: I don't know what you're talking about.

MEMÉ: Dami, give the stuff back to the hospital. Don't fight, you two.

VERÓNICA: Look, you can do whatever you want. But you can't do this to me. Okay?

GABI: Damián. Give it to her.

DAMIÁN: Stay out of this.

GRANDMOTHER: What's going on?

VERÓNICA: Nothing, Grandma. Damián got confused.

DAMIÁN: I don't bug you.

VERÓNICA: And I don't screw you over.

GABI: Relax, Verónica. Don't worry. He won't take anything.

VERÓNICA: I want him to give me the backpack now.

GABI: He's not going to give it to you, get it? But he won't take anything.

GRANDMOTHER: Verónica, calm down.

VERÓNICA: Give it to Gabi.

GABI: Give it to me. Is that okay?

VERÓNICA: Give it to Gabi or to Grandma, or else you're not leaving. Is that clear?

GABI: He'll give it to me, Vero. Calm down.

The DOCTOR *enters.*

DOCTOR: Good morning. How's the belle of the ball?

VERÓNICA: Eduardo, I'm sorry but I couldn't get to the phone last night.

DOCTOR: That's what I figured.

MEMÉ: Are you the doctor?

DOCTOR: That's right.

MARITO: I'm bleeding to death, doctor.

DOCTOR: What happened?

GABI: Nothing, no big deal.

DOCTOR: Let me see. It's a nasty cut. Does it hurt?

The DOCTOR *touches the wound.* MARITO *screams.*

DOCTOR: That's normal. We can put a bandage on it later if you like, Verónica.

VERÓNICA: Yes, whatever you think is best.

DAMIÁN: I'm leaving.

DOCTOR: Damián, right?

DAMIÁN: Yes.

DOCTOR: Can you stay a while longer?

GABI: What for?

DOCTOR: You can't complain, Grandma. You have all this family to take care of you.

GRANDMOTHER: So can I leave, doctor?

DOCTOR: No. Not yet.

GABI: What's wrong with her?

VERÓNICA: Calm down, Gabi.

DOCTOR: I have a few concerns, so I'll take this opportunity with all the family here.

VERÓNICA: Of course. No problem.

DOCTOR: Some routine questions.

VERÓNICA: Great.

DOCTOR: Your grandmother was taking some pills, right?

MEMÉ: Yes, some pink ones.

GABI: Sleeping pills.

MARITO: Diuretics.

VERÓNICA: Grandma takes diuretics?

GABI: No.

MARITO: Yes.

DOCTOR: It seems to me that they were diuretics.

GABI: I thought they were sleeping pills!

MARITO: They're diuretics, Gabi.

DOCTOR: And who prescribed these diuretics?

MEMÉ: The physician.

GABI: A doctor, I assume. Why?

DOCTOR: When did he prescribe them and what for? If you remember…

GABI: Mom.

MEMÉ: I don't know. It was a long time ago.

VERÓNICA: What were they for?

MEMÉ: I think they were for dizziness. Grandma tends to get dizzy.

VERÓNICA: Were the pills bad, Eduardo?

MARITO: They're expired.

DOCTOR: The doctor's name?

They look at each other. Nobody knows the answer.

MARITO: Dami gets them for free at the pharmacy.

VERÓNICA: Not for free. They're paid for.

GABI: Yes, they're paid for.

DOCTOR: Without a prescription?

MARITO: Dami gets them for free.

MEMÉ: Doctor Chipola or Chipoletti…

DOCTOR: Did anyone else in the household take pills?

MEMÉ: No, nobody else.

GABI: You take them, Mom! And you give them to Marito too!

MEMÉ: We give them to him…! You give them to him too!

DAMIÁN: Why all these questions, doctor? I don't understand.

DOCTOR: And, Damián, you are…?

DAMIÁN: Her grandson.

DOCTOR: Ah. You're all her grandchildren.

MEMÉ: No, I'm her daughter.

DOCTOR: Merced.

MEMÉ: Memé.

DOCTOR: You're her daughter.

MEMÉ: Yes. Why?

DOCTOR: So, you're the mother of…

VERÓNICA: She is everyone's mother, Eduardo.

DOCTOR: Oh. Everyone's. But the last names…?

GABI: We don't all have the same father.

DOCTOR: Yes, of course, but…

VERÓNICA: What's the confusion?

DOCTOR: Whose last name is Coleman?

GABI: Grandma and Marito.

DOCTOR: Grandma and Marito.

GABI: They're Colemans.

DOCTOR: Of course, Marito is from another marriage.

MARITO: No, same marriage.

MEMÉ: How many marriages do you think I had?

GRANDMOTHER: None, doctor.

GABI: Verónica and Marito have the same father.

DOCTOR: But…

VERÓNICA: But we don't have the same last name.

MARITO: I'm a Coleman.

VERÓNICA: I'm a Zanelli.

DOCTOR: Zanelli?

MEMÉ: With a "z."

VERÓNICA: Zanelli-Toker. Toker is my married name.

MEMÉ: Her husband's.

DOCTOR: Her married name.

GABI: Memé's a Fortuna.

MARITO (*to* DOCTOR): Her name is Blanca Merced Fortuna.

MEMÉ: Memé.

DOCTOR: Who's left?

GABI: Damián and I are Müllers.

DOCTOR: Müller... Müller isn't...

GABI & VERÓNICA (*almost in unison*): It's the last name of Grandma's second husband.

DAMIÁN: Any problem?

DOCTOR: No, as a doctor, I just needed to learn the family structure. That's all.

MEMÉ: A normal family, like any other, with their issues. Write that down.

MARITO: Doctor, last night my mom stabbed me in the arm with a knife.

MEMÉ: I didn't mean to. Just playing with the knife.

DOCTOR: Him or you?

MEMÉ: What?

DOCTOR: Who was playing?

MEMÉ: Both of us. We were playing around.

GABI: It wasn't on purpose.

MARITO: Yes, it was, doctor. She wants to kick me out of bed.

DOCTOR: Really?

DAMIÁN: What is this for?

MARITO: She wants to sleep alone.

DOCTOR: And you don't want that?

MARITO: Yes, me too.

VERÓNICA: They don't sleep in the same bed, Eduardo!

MARITO: Yes.

DOCTOR: Yes or no.

VERÓNICA: No.

GABI: Yes.

DAMIÁN: Gabi!

VERÓNICA: They do?

GABI: Yes, they sleep in the same bed.

VERÓNICA: This is news to me.

DAMIÁN: What does this matter now?

DOCTOR: What do you think?

GABI: It's always been like that. They don't like sleeping apart.

DAMIÁN: I am asking what this has to do with Grandma!

VERÓNICA: I didn't know Mario and Memé slept in the same bed.

DOCTOR: Do you sleep alone?

GABI: Yes.

MEMÉ: Yes, she has her own room and sleeps alone; he (*meaning* DAMIÁN) has his own room and sleeps alone, and Grandma has her own room and sleeps alone, and we also have our own room, and we sleep together. And there's no TV at home. Write that down too.

DOCTOR: But why?

MEMÉ: Why what?

DOCTOR: Is there any reason why you sleep together?

MEMÉ: It just happened.

MARITO: It's nicer.

GABI: They don't want to sleep apart, doctor.

DAMIÁN: That's enough, Gabi.

GABI: It's true; it's true.

MARITO: She gets scared, doctor. She says Grandma's going to have us committed.

DOCTOR: Really?

MEMÉ: No, that was before.

MARITO: That she'll put us in a hospital. Awake, but locked up.

DAMIÁN: Shut up, Mario!

MARITO: That's what she says.

MEMÉ: Not anymore. That was before, doctor. Now everything's normal.

GABI: Mom isn't entirely mature, doctor.

DOCTOR: She isn't?

MEMÉ: Why not?

GABI: Because, Mom! Haven't you noticed?

VERÓNICA: Excuse me, Eduardo. I think this has nothing to do with Grandma's case.

DOCTOR: Nothing at all?

MARITO: Now, when Grandma dies, there will be a spare room for me.

VERÓNICA: Excuse me, Gabi, but let's be sure to explain that both Marito and Memé are capable of saying anything that pops into their heads.

GABI: That's true.

DOCTOR: But they sleep together.

MEMÉ: Yes.

GABI: Yes.

VERÓNICA: Well, I didn't know that.

MARITO: The house is sinking, doctor. Memé can't hold it up, and Gabi and Damián are leaving, and Verónica isn't there, and Grandma is dead.

GABI: Grandma is alive, Marito! What are you talking about?

MARITO: But for how much longer, Gabi?

DOCTOR: Fine, this is enough for me.

MARITO: There's more, doctor.

DAMIÁN *hits* MARITO*'s back to silence him.*

DOCTOR: Tomorrow we'll have the results and we'll know what's going on. I was interested in learning about Leonarda's background.

MEMÉ: Gabi's been in charge of pills in general.

DOCTOR: That's fine. I'll leave you to yourselves.

VERÓNICA: I'll call you later, Eduardo.

DOCTOR: Of course. Later I want to take a look at that wound, Mario.

MARITO: No.

MEMÉ: I'll take him.

DOCTOR: Okay, I'll be waiting.

The DOCTOR *exits.*

GABI: Grandma, are you okay?

GRANDMOTHER: Yes.

GABI: You'll see. Tomorrow they'll have the lab results. Everything will be fine, and you'll be able to come home.

DAMIÁN: See you tomorrow, Grandma.

DAMIÁN *leaves in a hurry.*

VERÓNICA: Damián! Damián!

GABI *stops her.* VERÓNICA *goes to the bathroom.*

MEMÉ: Come, Marito, let's go see the doctor, so he can look at your hand and fix it.

MARITO: Memé, I think I'm going to stay here tonight, you know? I think my presence will be needed.

MEMÉ: Yes, I think I'm staying too.

MARITO: Both of us will stay.

MEMÉ: Yes. Let's go see the doctor.

MARITO *and* MEMÉ *exit. At the same time, the* DOCTOR *comes in, through the bathroom, with the saline solution.* GABI *exits through the door. The second day turns smoothly into the third day.*

DAY THREE:

DOCTOR: Let's have a look, Grandma. Good. Today we're going to run the last of the tests. We'll go to the lab, and then we won't bother you anymore.

GRANDMOTHER: Can I leave then?

DOCTOR: Not yet. You're not eating. I can't make any promises.

GRANDMOTHER: Can't they let me share the room with another patient, at least? I'm bored here.

DOCTOR: And your family? Aren't they coming by today?

GRANDMOTHER: I can't expect them to set up house here. They have their own commitments.

DOCTOR: You have a beautiful family. I mean it.

GRANDMOTHER: A little strange.

DOCTOR: Verónica wasn't raised at home with you, right?

GRANDMOTHER: No, her father behaved very well with her.

DOCTOR: But the family bond was preserved?

GRANDMOTHER: Yes, but she's very busy. Her job, her house…

DOCTOR: The children. You have beautiful great-grandchildren.

GRANDMOTHER: I do? I haven't met them, but they must be lovely.

DOCTOR: You haven't met them?

GRANDMOTHER: No.

DOCTOR: May I ask why not?

GRANDMOTHER: No.

DOCTOR: Strange about them, isn't it?

GRANDMOTHER: What's strange about who?

DOCTOR: Verónica and Mario.

GRANDMOTHER: What's so strange?

DOCTOR: I mean, the same father gives one his last name but not the other...

GRANDMOTHER: Doctor, if that doesn't bother us, why should it bother you?

GABI, DAMIÁN, MEMÉ, *and* MARITO *enter.*

GABI: Hello!

MEMÉ: Mom, they took out the tube!

DOCTOR: Yes, we removed her IV.

GABI: Is everything okay, doctor?

DOCTOR: She won't eat. We should keep an eye on her because she could grow weaker.

MEMÉ: You've got to eat, Mommy, or else we'll never leave this place.

GABI: What's wrong, Grandma? Aren't you hungry?

GRANDMOTHER: Have a taste of what I'm being fed, and then you tell me.

MARITO: At least you get to eat, Grandma. There's nothing left at home, doctor. No more cans.

DAMIÁN: Shut your mouth, Mario!

MARITO: The oven doesn't even work.

GABI: It works. Recently it hasn't been running.

MEMÉ: They shut off the gas.

GRANDMOTHER: They shut off the gas?

MARITO: We're freezing there.

GRANDMOTHER: Why did they shut it off, Gabi?

GABI: You always paid the bill, so nobody noticed, and it was shut off. We'll take care of it.

MEMÉ: Yeah? With what money?

MARITO: Nobody bathes in that house.

DAMIÁN: Come, Marito. Be quiet and eat this, okay?

DAMIÁN *points at something in his backpack.*

MEMÉ: Doctor, I wanted to ask you something. You wouldn't happen to have a few extra pills?

DOCTOR: Pills?

MEMÉ: Because mine ran out.

DOCTOR: I don't know what kind of pills you take.

MEMÉ: Pills, to avoid winding up…

DOCTOR: Contraceptives.

MEMÉ: Yes. I need some.

GRANDMOTHER: You take birth-control pills?

MEMÉ: A little late, but I learned my lesson.

GABI: Mom, please, don't.

MEMÉ: But Gabi, he's a doctor! He has to get free samples. Or are you going to buy them for me?

DOCTOR: It's no bother. I'll get you some.

GABI: There's no need, doctor.

DOCTOR: No problem. And you, Marito? How's your wound?

MARITO: It's got gangrene.

GABI: That's not true, doctor. It's much better.

DOCTOR: I'd like to look at it later.

MARITO: No.

DOCTOR: I'll be back soon for the test. Bye.

GABI: Bye, doctor.

He exits.

MARITO: Who's first?

MEMÉ: I called dibs.

GABI: Hurry up, Memé!

GRANDMOTHER: What's going on?

GABI: Grandma, since the gas got shut off, we can't bathe at home. Do you mind if we take a shower here?

GRANDMOTHER: Here?

GABI: Fast one!

GRANDMOTHER: Jesus...

GABI: Only if it's okay with you.

MEMÉ: We only have cold water at home, Mom.

GRANDMOTHER: But hurry up. Before Verónica gets here!

DAMIÁN: Go, hurry up, Memé!

MARITO: Hurry up, Memé, hurry up!

MEMÉ: Is there shampoo in the bathroom?

GABI: I brought some. Take this.

MEMÉ: But this is the one from home. Isn't there a softer one?

GABI: No, Memé!

MEMÉ: Have you seen what it does to my hair?

GABI: Go bathe, Mom.

MEMÉ: Is there any conditioner?

DAMIÁN: Go take your shower!

MEMÉ: Watch over your brother, Gabi!

GABI: Nothing will happen, Grandma.

MEMÉ: The last straw.

She goes into the bathroom.

MARITO: What's this button for?

GABI: I don't know. Don't push it, or else the nurses will come.

MARITO: And this one?

GABI: I don't know. Take a look, Damián.

DAMIÁN: How would I know what it's for?

GABI: Go see if anyone's coming!

MARITO: What is this button for, Gabi?

GABI: I don't know! Don't push it, just in case.

MEMÉ (*from the bathroom*): There's no soap.

GABI: Really?

MEMÉ (*entering*): I swear. I checked.

GABI: Okay, start washing your hair and I'll get some soap.

DAMIÁN: Take this.

GABI: Did you bring some?

DAMIÁN: More or less.

He hands GABI *a bar of soap.*

GABI: This one is the hospital's. Where did you get it from?

DAMIÁN: Room 512.

GABI: Oh, Dami, please, be careful.

GRANDMOTHER: Who's going to get upset about some soap?

MEMÉ: And a comb.

GABI: Didn't you bring a comb?

MEMÉ: No.

They look at DAMIÁN.

DAMIÁN: I'll go get one.

GABI: No, you stay here and you start your shower. I'll go get a comb…

GABI *exits.* MEMÉ *goes into the bathroom.*

MARITO: Dami, the sandwich. Make sure nobody comes in.

DAMIÁN *gives him a wrapped sandwich.*

MARITO: Excuse me, Grandma.

He gets on the bed.

DAMIÁN: Get off the bed.

GRANDMOTHER: Let him. But careful!

MARITO (*unwraps the sandwich and starts eating*): What time do you eat?

GRANDMOTHER: In a while. (*Pause.*) What's that?

MARITO: Sandwich.

GRANDMOTHER: Give me some?

MARITO: Why?

GRANDMOTHER: I'm hungry.

MARITO: Me too.

GRANDMOTHER: Be nice.

MARITO: You can't eat this, Grandma.

GRANDMOTHER: Just a little bit. I'm fine.

MARITO: No. It's harmful to your health.

GRANDMOTHER: Damián, tell him.

DAMIÁN: Can you eat that, Grandma?

GRANDMOTHER: A little bit. I'm better.

DAMIÁN: Give it to her.

MARITO: No.

DAMIÁN: Give it to her, Mario!

MARITO: Why?

DAMIÁN grabs him. They struggle on the bed, and DAMIÁN takes the sandwich from MARITO. GABI enters with a comb and walks to the bathroom. GRANDMOTHER takes a bite out of the sandwich and hides it under the sheets.

GABI: I got a comb. Take it, Memé.

She leaves the bathroom.

GABI (*to DAMIÁN*): Are you next?

DAMIÁN: No, you go.

MEMÉ enters, combing her hair.

MEMÉ: What joy, warm water!

GABI: Okay. I'm going now. Keep an eye out that nobody's coming.

MEMÉ: It's great to be here, after all.

GABI (*from the bathroom*): Mom! (*Reappears.*) You can't wash your clothes here! You left your panties hanging up!

MEMÉ: They were dirty. What do you want me to do?

GABI: You're not home, you're not home!

She tosses the panties at MEMÉ and goes back in the bathroom.

MEMÉ: I know I'm not home! There's warm water here! You're kind of moronic today, Gabi!

MEMÉ hangs the panties from the IV pole.

DAMIÁN: Put your shoes on, Mom, now!

MEMÉ: Why don't you all get off my back and take care of your sick Grandma instead?

MARITO: Grandma's doing better.

VERÓNICA enters.

VERÓNICA: Excuse me. Is it possible that four extra lunches were ordered from this room? They gave me a bill for four extra lunches. I'd like to think it's the hospital's mistake, right?

DAMIÁN: No, we ordered them.

VERÓNICA: Are you all nuts?

MEMÉ: There's nothing left at home.

VERÓNICA: Couldn't you have asked me first?

DAMIÁN: You weren't around for us to ask you, Verónica.

MARITO: We're too hungry to fool around with questions.

MEMÉ: It was a desperate situation, Vero.

VERÓNICA: Okay. It's done. How are you, Grandma?

GRANDMOTHER: Better.

MARITO: She's hungry.

VERÓNICA: Good! Eduardo said you wouldn't eat.

GRANDMOTHER: I ate a little.

MARITO: I didn't.

MEMÉ: Me neither.

DAMIÁN: We'll eat soon.

VERÓNICA: All I am asking for is that you let me know, or at least, ask me, because, frankly, everything's really expensive here. It's done; it's not important.

She sees MEMÉ's *panties dangling and notices her hair is wet.*

VERÓNICA: Memé, did you take a shower here?

MEMÉ: It was Gabi's idea.

DAMIÁN: They shut off the gas at home.

VERÓNICA: They shut off the gas?

MARITO: Our situation is disgraceful, Verónica.

VERÓNICA: Didn't Gabi come today?

MEMÉ: Yes.

VERÓNICA: Where is she?

MEMÉ: She's busy right now.

VERÓNICA: Doing what?

MARITO: She's making use of the facilities.

VERÓNICA: Gabi too?

DAMIÁN (*walks to the bathroom*): Gabi, Verónica's here.

Pause. GABI *enters with her hair wet.*

GABI: Hi, Vero. I am sorry, but they shut off the gas and…

VERÓNICA: It's fine. No problem. Look, I've been thinking. This is an unusual situation for me.

GABI: For all of us.

VERÓNICA: Yes, I suppose for you too. It's …

MEMÉ: Odd.

VERÓNICA: It's like circumstances are forcing us to live together. (DAMIÁN *tries to leave.*) Dami, one moment, please. So I think it can be an opportunity for us to talk.

MARITO *gets up on* GRANDMOTHER's *bed to sit on the other side.*

MARITO: I think that a family chat is good.

GABI: Mario, what are you doing? Get off the bed!

VERÓNICA: These things. For instance, I find these things odd.

MARITO: They're panties hanging up to dry.

VERÓNICA *removes the panties from the pole and* MARITO *takes them.*

VERÓNICA: I know. I won't criticize: everyone lives the way they do. Frankly, who am I to judge?

MARITO: Actually, nobody.

GABI: It's a difficult situation for us too.

VERÓNICA: What I mean to say is that I have my life set up in a particular way; but I still want us to be able to get to know each other and understand…

MARITO: Memé takes contraceptives.

MEMÉ: All us girls do, Mario.

VERÓNICA: Perhaps my position seems more comfortable and straightforward, because I have a family that is... I won't say normal, but more...

MEMÉ: Average. An average family.

VERÓNICA: More conventional. Anyway, I didn't choose to leave Grandma's house. You don't decide at the age of one where you'll live, or who with. Others decided for me; no question about it, right?

GABI: Yes.

MEMÉ: But you ended up better off.

DAMIÁN: I don't know if she ended up better off.

MEMÉ: Yes, she ended up better off.

DAMIÁN: I said I don't know.

MARITO: Yes, she ended up better off, Dami.

VERÓNICA: Anyway, I don't think the issue is who ended up better off. For a five- or six-year-old girl, to be asked about her mommy and not know how to answer... Nothing against you, Memé.

MEMÉ: Of course not!

VERÓNICA: It's not a happy situation. I wouldn't wish it on my own children.

MEMÉ: No, me neither. It just happened that way.

VERÓNICA: Yes, of course.

GABI: I'm not sure where you're headed with this.

VERÓNICA: Since it would appear that it's my obligation to be financially responsible for everything... I wanted to explain that it isn't my obligation but rather...

MEMÉ: A pleasure.

VERÓNICA: A decision. A wish.

MARITO: Vero, I'm hungry.

MEMÉ: Me too!

DAMIÁN: The food's on its way.

VERÓNICA: No. Sorry, but I had to cancel the food.

MARITO: Fucking bitch!

VERÓNICA: I'll give you some money and you can get something to eat nearby!

DAMIÁN: Why?

VERÓNICA: It has to do with what we were talking about. Grandma's always asking to meet the children, and… I arranged with Patricio for him to bring them here at noon.

GRANDMOTHER: Really? How wonderful!

VERÓNICA: Yes, they're on their way.

MEMÉ: The kids are coming? That's terrific!

MARITO: I don't think they'll let them in.

GABI: Cut it out, Mario!

VERÓNICA: I believe it's appropriate.

GABI: Yes. Are you happy, Grandma?

GRANDMOTHER: What do you think?

VERÓNICA: So, I thought, that is, I think, it would be best for us to leave Grandma to meet her great-grandchildren calmly.

Silence.

VERÓNICA: I don't know if it's good to have so many people around when they arrive. That's what I thought.

DAMIÁN: Do you want us to leave?

MEMÉ: Oh, Dami… How can we leave without meeting them?

VERÓNICA: For a first meeting, I thought it was best to have Grandma calm.

MEMÉ: And me?

VERÓNICA: Later we'll see, Mom.

GABI: I don't think anything bad's going to happen if we stay with Grandma.

VERÓNICA: I'd feel more comfortable if Grandma were by herself.

GABI: Why?

MARITO: Because she's ashamed of the midgets.

MEMÉ: Knock it off with the midgets, Mario!

VERÓNICA: Now do you realize why?

GABI: I thought you said that we had to avoid judging each other, to accept each other the way we are, and so on...

VERÓNICA: Yes, let's accept that I want my children to meet Grandma in a calm environment.

MEMÉ: We'll stay calm. We can give Marito a few drops!

VERÓNICA: I don't think it is too much to ask. So now you're all dying to stay at the hospital forever?

GABI: What do you think, Grandma?

GRANDMOTHER: Vero, I think it would be nicer if we all meet them.

VERÓNICA: No. I won't expose my children and my husband to an embarrassing situation!

DAMIÁN: If you're embarrassed, don't bring them!

VERÓNICA: I'm not embarrassed!

DAMIÁN: Yes, you're embarrassed!

VERÓNICA: Yes, I am embarrassed, and you'd be embarrassed too!

DAMIÁN: What are you talking about?

VERÓNICA: I didn't mean "embarrassed." I meant "afraid." All I want is Grandma to be calm. That's all.

MARITO: I don't think Grandma's going to be calm with two midgets running around here.

VERÓNICA: I refuse to bring my children if this lunatic is around!

DAMIÁN: I'm not leaving.

VERÓNICA: Gabi, you're reasonable.

GABI: You're not being reasonable!

MEMÉ: Let's be reasonable. What's the problem? Is it Marito? If Marito's the problem, he can go and the children can come.

MARITO: No, Marito stays.

GABI: I can't accept that.

VERÓNICA: Are you staying?

GABI: I won't be a party to this.

DAMIÁN: Marito stays and so do I.

MEMÉ: You see what they're like! What are we going to do, Vero?

VERÓNICA (*takes the cell phone out*): Hello, Patricio. It's me. At the hospital. Are you on your way? No, don't come. No, it's just a complicated morning. No, no. Yes, yes. Okay, thanks. Yes, that's better. Bye. (*Hangs up.*) Sorry, Grandma, but it's my family.

Pause. HERNÁN *enters.* DAMIÁN *goes into the bathroom.*

HERNÁN: Excuse me. Am I intruding?

MEMÉ: No, it's just us. Come in.

VERÓNICA: Hernán.

GABI: Sit down, if you want.

HERNÁN (*to* GRANDMOTHER): How's your health?

GRANDMOTHER: Perfect. Your marital status?

HERNÁN: Untouched.

GRANDMOTHER: There's hope, Gabi!

GABI: Grandma!

HERNÁN: No, Grandma. You'll scare her away from me that way.

GRANDMOTHER: Young people are so slow...

HERNÁN: Well, this is just like barbequing: you have to take it slow so that it doesn't scorch.

VERÓNICA: Did I call you?

HERNÁN: No, I was going around in the car and thought I'd drop by to see how your grandmother was doing.

MARITO: Were you bringing the midgets?

HERNÁN: No. I thought they're with their father, right?

VERÓNICA: So you answer for my children when someone asks about midgets?

HERNÁN: Sorry, I thought it was some kind of family code.

VERÓNICA: No code. Okay, Hernán? No code.

The DOCTOR *enters.* DAMIÁN *comes out the bathroom.*

DOCTOR: Grandma, we need to go for a walk.

VERÓNICA: Eduardo, are you taking her?

DOCTOR: Yes. We need to run some tests. We'll be a while.

GABI: Come on, Grandma. Let me help you.

GRANDMOTHER *starts singing while she gets out of bed and sits on a chair.*

GRANDMOTHER: Poor unlucky woman, she forgot to breathe. Poor unlucky woman, now she's in her grave.

MEMÉ: Don't you want to change your nightgown, Mom?

GRANDMOTHER: Which one did you bring?

GABI: The beige one you like, with buttons, Grandma. If not, you also have the one Vero brought.

VERÓNICA: Yes, it's in the bathroom.

MARITO *and* MEMÉ *lie down on the bed.*

GRANDMOTHER: No. It doesn't matter.

GABI: Sure, Grandma?

GRANDMOTHER: It doesn't matter. Look, when my cousin Raquel was getting married, she asked her mother, "What should I wear on my wedding night?" She said, "Wear a thick flannel robe up to your chin." She didn't like that idea much. So she asked her best friend, who said, "Wear a short see-through negligee, with a neckline down to your navel." She still wasn't convinced. Then she asked me, "Leonarda, what do I do?" "Look," I said, "it doesn't matter. Whatever you put on, they're gonna fuck you anyway." Whenever you wish, doctor.

DOCTOR: Let's go.

The DOCTOR *takes* GRANDMOTHER *away.* MARITO *finds the sandwich between the sheets and starts to eat it. Silence.*

HERNÁN: She's one heck of a woman, huh? Look, I never knew my grandmothers, but I would have loved for them to be like her. So fun and alive.

VERÓNICA *and* GABI *cry.* DAMIÁN *exits the room.*

HERNÁN: But don't be down. Just think how she has all her family all around her. So much love, everybody together. (VERÓNICA *goes into the bathroom.*) Really, it's a beautiful family.

MEMÉ: Shut up, please! (*Pause.*) Okay, it's over!

VERÓNICA *enters the room talking on the phone.*

VERÓNICA: Hello, Patricio. No, fine. They have just taken Grandma to run some tests. I think it'll take a while. I don't know when I'll head home. Yes, that's better. No, no, I'll grab something on my own, really. Love you. Bye. (*To* HERNÁN) Are you on a job now?

HERNÁN: No. I'm just driving around.

VERÓNICA: Shall we go?

HERNÁN: Sure. I'll give you a lift, Vero.

VERÓNICA (*to the rest of them*): I'm… leaving.

She exits.

HERNÁN: Well, off to work. (*To* GABI) Do you know if you're staying here tonight?

GABI: I don't know. I guess so.

HERNÁN: May I keep you company? Here. I'd really like to.

GABI: If you feel like it, stop by.

VERÓNICA (*entering*): Shall we, Hernán?

HERNÁN: Yes. (*To* GABI) I'll stop by, then.

MARITO: Bye, darling.

HERNÁN *exits with* VERÓNICA.

MARITO: Memé, I am really, really, really hungry.

The DOCTOR *and* GRANDMOTHER *enter.*

DOCTOR: Well, here we are. That wasn't so terrible, was it?

MARITO: Did they put you inside some dark pipe, Grandma?

GRANDMOTHER: No. They only took some X-rays.

DOCTOR: And Verónica?

GABI: She left.

MARITO: She left with the…

GABI: She had things to do.

DOCTOR: No problem, I'll call her later. Marito, I need you to come with me to the lab.

MARITO: Why?

DOCTOR: I wanted to check the results of your blood test.

GABI: Is everything okay?

DOCTOR: Yes, just routine. Sometimes, because of coagulation, it's better to run tests a second time.

MARITO: Are they going to draw blood?

DOCTOR: Yes.

MARITO: But they drew some a little while ago, doctor.

DOCTOR: Don't worry. You still have plenty of blood left.

MARITO: But I didn't eat anything today.

DOCTOR: You'll eat something now in the Emergency Room.

MARITO: Oh, okay.

MARITO *tosses the rest of the sandwich. They exit.*

MEMÉ: Come on, Mommy, to bed!

GRANDMOTHER: Will you help me to the bathroom, Gabi?

GABI: Dim the lights, Memé.

MEMÉ: We thought you weren't coming back, Mom.

GABI: That's not true, Memé.

GRANDMOTHER: I think Memé's right. I'm not going back home.

GABI: Don't say that, Grandma! Careful… slowly…

They go into the bathroom. MEMÉ *remains facing upstage for a moment and starts to put on her sweater. The fourth day begins.*

DAY FOUR:

MEMÉ: Gabi… Gabi, are you in the bathroom?

Nobody answers. MEMÉ *is about to leave the room when* VERÓNICA *comes out of the bathroom.*

VERÓNICA: Memé!

MEMÉ: Vero, you were in the bathroom!

VERÓNICA: Yes, I was seeing nothing was left behind.

MEMÉ: It looks like someone's moving.

VERÓNICA: Yes. I think we should clear the room now.

MEMÉ: Why don't we take advantage of being left alone to talk a little? Since we're here. We never get to.

VERÓNICA: Do you think now is a good time? I think we should go.

MEMÉ: When, then?

VERÓNICA: Some other time.

MEMÉ: Vero, you see that I'm not lying when I say life at home is hell.

VERÓNICA: You add your own to the mix, Memé.

MEMÉ: Yes, I know I'm a mess, but now that Grandma won't be there I don't want to go back home.

VERÓNICA: Don't worry. Everything will be fine.

MEMÉ: You can't abandon me now!

VERÓNICA: I won't abandon you.

MEMÉ: Did you think about what we discussed the other day?

VERÓNICA: No, I said I wasn't going to think about it.

MEMÉ: Why?

VERÓNICA: I can't. Don't insist, Mom.

MEMÉ: Can't we at least make an attempt?

VERÓNICA: Can't you respect that I'm in mourning, Mom, please?

A sound coming from the bathroom is heard.

MEMÉ: Were you with someone in the bathroom?

The DOCTOR *comes out of the bathroom.*

DOCTOR: One of Leonarda's nightgowns was left in here, Verónica. Uh, Memé, what's up?

VERÓNICA: How about that? It was right there and I didn't even see it.

DOCTOR: Well, I'll take it.

VERÓNICA: No, give it to me.

DOCTOR: Yes, of course.

VERÓNICA: Do you want to take it home, Mom?

DOCTOR: I'll continue my rounds. There's no rush to clear the room.

VERÓNICA: We were leaving anyway.

DOCTOR: Oh! Since you're here, Memé, I'd like to talk to you about something. You too, Verónica. Please, take a seat.

VERÓNICA: What is it?

DOCTOR: It's about Mario's blood work. It's not good.

VERÓNICA: Why… what?

DOCTOR: I thought there was something strange with the first test, so I ordered a second one and…

VERÓNICA: Is there something wrong with him?

DOCTOR: Leukemia. There's a 99 percent chance that it's leukemia. We need to perform a spinal tap to prove definitively that's what's

wrong with him. I don't know if the idea is to have him treated here.
We could have him admitted to get a jump on the problem.

VERÓNICA: Hold on. All at once, like this… It's too much.

DOCTOR: Of course, but any time we can gain now is crucial.

VERÓNICA: I have to talk to Patricio…

MARITO *enters eating something from a hospital plate.*

DOCTOR: Marito! We were just talking about you.

MARITO: Why?

DOCTOR: No reason. Excuse me.

The DOCTOR *exits.*

VERÓNICA: What are you eating, Mario?

MARITO: Brains.

VERÓNICA: I don't believe you.

MARITO *shows her.*

VERÓNICA: Gross! They're brains.

MARITO: They're good for the blood. And my blood…

VERÓNICA: Really?

MARITO: They need to put it all back again. They need to take out all my
blood and put it back again.

VERÓNICA: Is that what the doctor told you?

MARITO: Not me. Why?

MEMÉ: Mario, your sister wants to talk to you.

MEMÉ *exits.*

VERÓNICA: How are you?

MARITO: Why?

VERÓNICA: Well, Grandma…

MARITO: It's over.

VERÓNICA: Really?

MARITO: There are worse things in life, Verónica.

VERÓNICA: Mario, I would like us to talk calmly.

MARITO: We've got to support Gabi. She's crying. I just saw her. She's crying in the hallway. I'm not; I'll do my crying some other time.

VERÓNICA: If you want to cry now...

MARITO: I'll cry some other time, Verónica. Now, we need to take care of things back home, settle the bedroom issue.

VERÓNICA: I would like to be close to all of you now.

MARITO: There are no more free rooms at home. Everything is taken.

VERÓNICA: You like making me mad, and, the worse thing is I'm so gullible that you always get to me.

MARITO: Are you going to leave the kids?

VERÓNICA: See? I especially don't like talking to you about my kids.

MARITO: Why?

VERÓNICA: Because you've got some kind of obsession with my kids.

MARITO: I love them very much. Very much, I love them.

VERÓNICA: I appreciate it, but since you don't know them, I find it hard to believe you love them so much.

MARITO: I do know them. I know both of them.

VERÓNICA: Anyway, it's not the kids I want to talk about.

MARITO: I do.

VERÓNICA: I repeat: I don't want to.

MARITO: They're really little, aren't they?

VERÓNICA: How have you been feeling lately?

MARITO: Especially the youngest. He is really tiny.

VERÓNICA: Mario, how have you been feeling?

MARITO: You say they're not midgets, but I think they are, because they're so small.

VERÓNICA: They're three and four years old. Their height's average for their age.

MARITO: I don't think so. I would have them checked, Verónica. They're really tiny.

VERÓNICA: Look, Mario, that's not the subject here.

MARITO: If you could keep only one, which one would you choose? Choose.

VERÓNICA: What?

MARITO: Choose one. Choose one.

Pause.

MARITO: You already chose one, Vero.

VERÓNICA: Mario.

MARITO: Would you feel bad keeping only one?

VERÓNICA: I have both my kids, and I don't need to keep only one of them.

MARITO: Then take better care of them.

VERÓNICA: What are you saying?

MARITO: Today, for example, wasn't a good day to go to the park. It rained, light, but it rained. You can't take the kids to the park. They'll get sick.

VERÓNICA: How do you know?

MARITO: Big mistake. Taking the midgets out today was a big mistake.

VERÓNICA: You're making things up, Mario. I was here all day. I didn't go to the park with my kids. I didn't even see them.

MARITO: No, you didn't. Not you, Verónica.

VERÓNICA: No, this is too much for me; you all sort it out.

She exits. She comes back looking for her cell phone in her bag.

VERÓNICA: Wait. Let's put an end to this madness. (*Pause.*) Hello, Guada. Yes, it's me. Yes, thanks. No, she didn't suffer. Thank you. Are the children with you? Great. Did you go anywhere today? Okay, okay. No, no problem. Great. Better if you do it, thanks. Bye. (*Hangs up. To* MARITO) Lies, Mario, all lies.

She goes over to him.

VERÓNICA: Listen to me...

MARITO: Did they or didn't they go?

VERÓNICA: ... because I'm talking to you seriously.

MARITO: They did.

VERÓNICA: You don't know me.

MARITO: You're a very bad mother, Verónica.

VERÓNICA: You don't have any idea who I am.

MARITO: A terrible mother.

VERÓNICA: Mario, I don't want to see you anywhere near my kids ever.

MARITO: I love them very much. That's why I take care of them.

VERÓNICA: You freak, you fucking lunatic! I'll kill you, Mario. You got that? I'll kill you!

MARITO *grabs her and throws her onto the bed.*

MARITO: And I'll kill you, you fucking bitch! I'm going to kill you right now!

VERÓNICA: Let go of me! Mario, let go of me!

GABI *and* HERNÁN *enter, followed by the* DOCTOR. MARITO *stands on top of the bed.* VERÓNICA *runs to the bathroom.*

GABI: Let go of her, Mario! Mario, stop!

MARITO (*jumps off the bed*): We have to go home, Gabi. Now! Let's go home!

VERÓNICA: Let him go, let him go!

GABI: Relax, Mario! There's paperwork to do. We'll go home after that.

DOCTOR: Can I help?

MARITO: We're leaving, doctor.

GABI: Calm down, Mario!

MARITO: I'll wait for you at home.

GABI: Enough, Mario!

MARITO *exits. Silence.*

DOCTOR: Have you talked to Verónica about Mario?

GABI: No. What happened?

DOCTOR: She's up to speed on everything. If you need me for anything, I'll be in the ER today.

GABI: Thanks for everything, doctor.

DOCTOR: You are welcome.

The DOCTOR *exits.*

GABI (*in the direction of the bathroom*): Verónica, are you okay?

Silence. GABI stores away some of GRANDMOTHER*'s things.*

HERNÁN: I can take the stuff to the car, if you like.

GABI: We'll see. Thanks.

HERNÁN: Gabi, will it be possible for us to see each other after all this?

GABI: I don't know, now…

HERNÁN: Sorry, you're right, now…

GABI: No, it didn't bother me…

HERNÁN: I'm afraid I'll never see you again, but if you tell me it's just a matter of time, I can wait as long as it takes.

VERÓNICA *comes out of the bathroom.*

VERÓNICA: And Eduardo?

GABI: He left. He said he knew something about Mario. Could that be?

VERÓNICA: About Mario? I haven't a clue.

GABI: Eduardo said you were up to speed on everything, Verónica.

VERÓNICA: Look, Gabi. All I know is I'm exhausted. Shall we go, Hernán?

HERNÁN: You didn't make an appointment today, Vero.

VERÓNICA: Where am I supposed to call?

HERNÁN: I don't have my car.

VERÓNICA: Oh, really?

HERNÁN: Actually, I have my car, but I'm not working.

VERÓNICA: Oh, okay. That's fine.

GABI: He's helping me a lot with Grandma.

HERNÁN: With the paperwork...

VERÓNICA: Yeah, Hernán's a sweetheart.

HERNÁN: Well, thanks.

GABI: I'm afraid I'm taking advantage of him, really.

VERÓNICA: Of him? No, he loves it.

HERNÁN: People taking advantage of me? I'm not so sure.

VERÓNICA: Not that they take advantage, but that they keep you in mind, I mean.

HERNÁN: I like to get involved, that's all.

VERÓNICA (*going over to* HERNÁN): Could you give me a lift home even though I didn't set it up?

HERNÁN: No, I can't.

VERÓNICA: It'd only take a moment.

HERNÁN: Sorry. I can't.

VERÓNICA: Are you serious?

GABI (*to* HERNÁN): Go. I can handle it.

HERNÁN: It's okay, don't worry. It's better, Vero...

VERÓNICA: Well, I guess it's better this way.

She tries to close her handbag but can't.

HERNÁN: Is it stuck?

VERÓNICA: Yes, but…

HERNÁN: I'll help you.

VERÓNICA: No, let go!

She trips over the IV pole while trying to get away from HERNÁN.

VERÓNICA: Shit! You can all go fuck yourselves!

She exits.

HERNÁN: I don't think she took it too well.

GABI: I'm not looking for anything.

HERNÁN: Uh huh.

GABI: But I like you.

HERNÁN: Uh huh.

GABI: I've had bad experiences up to now.

HERNÁN: Well, but that…

GABI: I don't want to suffer anymore.

HERNÁN: I get it.

GABI: No, not anymore.

HERNÁN: Never again.

DAMIÁN *enters.*

GABI: Dami! Where did you get yourself off to?

DAMIÁN (*referring to* HERNÁN): What's he doing here?

GABI: He's with me.

DAMIÁN: Tell him to leave.

GABI: Take it easy. He's looking after me.

DAMIÁN: Where's Grandma?

GABI: I wanted to talk to you, but I couldn't find you.

DAMIÁN: Is she sick?

Silence.

DAMIÁN: Did she die?

Silence. GABI *embraces him. He recoils.*

DAMIÁN: I need some money, Gabi. For a while.

GABI: What happened?

DAMIÁN: Doesn't matter. I need some money, that's all.

GABI: Okay. Take this. It's not much.

DAMIÁN: I'll pay you back later.

GABI: What do I do?

DAMIÁN: I'm going to disappear for a while.

GABI: For how long?

DAMIÁN: A while.

GABI: Can I see you?

DAMIÁN: No, better if you don't.

GABI: Will you call?

DAMIÁN: No. Sorry.

MEMÉ *enters.*

MEMÉ: Oh, Dami! Did you hear about Grandma? (*To* HERNÁN) Are you here with Verónica?

HERNÁN: No.

MEMÉ: If you see her, could you tell her to wait for me? I'll be in the bathroom.

HERNÁN: Sure, we'll let her know.

MEMÉ *goes into the bathroom.*

GABI: Let me check Grandma's bag.

HERNÁN: I have some money. Take this.

DAMIÁN: No.

HERNÁN: Take it, I said. It's cool.

DAMIÁN: Okay, but I'll pay you back.

GABI *finds* VERÓNICA*'s wallet on the bed.*

GABI: Isn't this Verónica's wallet?

DAMIÁN: Give it to me.

GABI *gives him the wallet.* DAMIÁN *takes the money and throws the wallet on the bed.*

DAMIÁN: I'm off. Take care of yourself.

DAMIÁN *exits. The others are silent.*

GABI: Do you have a place?

HERNÁN: Yes.

GABI: I'm not going back home. Memé and Verónica will take care of the house and Marito.

HERNÁN: Are you sure? Fine. Okay, let's go.

They exit together. At the same time, VERÓNICA *comes back in looking for her wallet.* MEMÉ *comes in from the bathroom.*

MEMÉ: Vero!

VERÓNICA: Memé!

MEMÉ: Are you leaving?

VERÓNICA: Yes.

MEMÉ: Vero.

VERÓNICA: What?

MEMÉ: Isn't there anything you want to tell me?

VERÓNICA: No.

MEMÉ: Sure?

VERÓNICA: I think this was quite a difficult day for all of us, Memé.

MEMÉ: And me? Imagine what's in store for me: going back home without Grandma.

VERÓNICA: Things will fall back into place. You'll see.

MEMÉ: No.

VERÓNICA: You'll see.

MEMÉ: No.

MEMÉ *sits on a chair and gestures to* VERÓNICA *to come closer.*

MEMÉ: Vero.

VERÓNICA: What?

MEMÉ: Oh, come on.

VERÓNICA: What?

MEMÉ: On my lap.

VERÓNICA: What?

MEMÉ: On Mommy's lap. Come on!

VERÓNICA *goes over to* MEMÉ *and sits on her lap.*

VERÓNICA: What do you want?

MEMÉ: You know what I want.

VERÓNICA: I already told you it's impossible. It's crazy.

MEMÉ: No. I think that if you wanted to, we could make it happen.

VERÓNICA: And Patricio?

MEMÉ: That's what I was wondering about. Does Patricio... know?

VERÓNICA: Mom.

MEMÉ: I didn't know things weren't so great between you two.

VERÓNICA: Everything's really great, okay?

MEMÉ: So? I get it. He's really handsome.

VERÓNICA: No.

MEMÉ: The doctor.

VERÓNICA: No, that's not it.

MEMÉ: Not that kid there. I think he's a little young for you.

VERÓNICA: You have no idea what you're talking about.

MEMÉ: It would be terrible. Terrible!

VERÓNICA: What would be terrible?

MEMÉ: Look, Vero. I'm capable of taking measures in a situation that seems contrary to my best interests.

VERÓNICA: Are you threatening me?

MEMÉ: Well... In a certain way, yes.

VERÓNICA: Would you really do that?

MEMÉ: What else can I do?

VERÓNICA: But how do I deal with this?

MEMÉ: Things will fall back into place. You'll see.

VERÓNICA: We can come up with something, if you want. But I don't want anything to do with Gabi, Damián... and especially not with Mario. I don't want anything to do with Mario.

MEMÉ: No. Look, Gabi and Damián will stay at home and take care of Marito.

VERÓNICA: It can't happen.

MEMÉ: You'll see, we'll get along!

VERÓNICA: Do you need to pick anything up there?

MEMÉ: No. New house, new life. New bed, new sheets, new pillows, new faucets. Everything new. Don't you think, Vero?

VERÓNICA: Let's go, Mom.

MEMÉ: Let's go.

They exit.

The scene goes silent. Gradually, the hospital disappears, and the house reappears. MARITO is sitting on the sofa, attentive to noises coming from the front door. He thinks he's heard something and goes out to see. There's nobody. He enters slowly and sits on the sofa and waits.

END OF PLAY

TRANSLATORS' NOTES

1.   Yapeyú is a street in the Boedo neighborhood of Buenos Aires. The indigenous term also refers to the birthplace of South American independence hero General José de San Martín.

2.   The original Spanish (*número de documento*) refers to Argentina's national identification document.

THIRD WING
(The Story of an Absurd Attempt)

a play by Claudio Tolcachir

(2008)

Translated by Jean Graham-Jones

Tercer Cuerpo. Photo by Giampaolo Samà/Timbre 4

Tercer cuerpo (la historia de un intento absurdo) premiered on 23 August 2008, in the Timbre 4 Theatre, Buenos Aires, Argentina. The production was cosponsored by the Santiago a Mil Festival (Santiago, Chile). The following cast and design team were involved:

SANDRA	Ana Garibaldi
MANUEL	Hernán Grinstein
SOFÍA	Magdalena Grondona
HÉCTOR	José María Marcos
MONI	Daniela Pal

Lighting Design:	Omar Possemato
Set Design:	Gonzalo Córdoba Estévez
Space Design:	Claudio Tolcachir
Assistant Direction:	Melisa Hermida
Executive Production:	Jonathan Zak & Maxime Seugé

Book and Direction:	Claudio Tolcachir

CHARACTERS

SANDRA

MONI

HECTOR

SOFIA

MANUEL

An open space. No divisions or walls. Center stage, a small, labyrinthine office is outlined by some furniture; it's crammed with papers, file cabinets, and other work-related objects. The office also functions as different spaces, sometimes simultaneously: the office, SOFIA and MANUEL's home, various cafés, a club, a doctor's office.

The actors are always onstage unless the stage directions require them to leave.

When onstage, the actors remain in character. When they're not in a scene, they simply wait or reposition themselves for their next scene.

SOFIA AND MANUEL'S HOME:

SOFIA: I woke up this morning and you were still sleeping. I love to watch you sleep. You're so peaceful, like a little orphan boy. You sleep all curled up. With your mouth open. Whenever I meet someone, even before saying a word to them, I imagine what it's like to watch them sleep. It's the only thing that can make me fall in love. I didn't imagine that about you. Or else I imagined you sleeping with your eyes open, on guard. The way you are in life. But when you're sleeping I can watch you without being afraid. Without me being afraid. Without you being afraid. I'm going to speak. No holding back. I know you don't like it. But I'm feeling brave today. I would like to take care of you forever. Keep you under my wing. Be here for you. Your world. Be your world. Hold on, I'm not done. Oh, now I've forgotten... It's just that I think about forever, I'm embarrassed to say it, but that's the way it is. I would like to die by your side. Live with you all my life. Let you sleep so I can watch you. I don't have any doubts. I'll stay with you, I'll hold you, and I'll stay with you my whole life. I love you.

MANUEL: Me... I don't know.

OFFICE:

SANDRA *enters.* MONI, *wrapped up in a coat and sitting behind a desk, gets up to greet her.*

SANDRA (*entering*): Sorry I'm late.

MONI: Don't worry. I already let them know you were running behind.

SANDRA: How did you know?

MONI: Just in case, to cover for you.

SANDRA: Well, thanks. Were you straightening things up?

MONI: The usual, I didn't touch your stuff, because you have your own way of doing things, but Hector's was a mess, since he's hardly ever here…

SANDRA: And if I hadn't gotten here late?

MONI: What?

SANDRA: How did you know I was running behind if I hadn't gotten here yet?

MONI: No. It's not that I knew, Sandy, I just figured. Call it intuition.

SANDRA: Look…

MONI: I've already had two cups of coffee. Nothing seems to warm me up.

SANDRA: Have you seen my calendar?

MONI: I put it in the drawer with the handle missing. Isn't that where you keep it?

SANDRA: No.

MONI: I don't want to catch cold, I haven't recovered from the last time.

SANDRA: Rushing here warmed me up.

MONI: Anyway, don't take your coat off yet; we've got to ask them to get us another office or get us a heater, or something.

SANDRA: I can't open it. Why did you put it away? It wasn't bothering anyone here.

MONI: Sorry, I don't like to touch your stuff.

SANDRA: I have my own way of doing things.

MONTI: Lift it from the side, you have a lot of stuff in that drawer.

SANDRA: That's why I don't use it.

MONI: But why don't you throw some of it out? You have papers in there from I don't know when.

SANDRA: Do you need this drawer for something?

MONI: No.

SANDRA: So...

MONI: Have you heard anything from Hector?

SANDRA: Did he call?

MONI: No.

SANDRA: Poor guy...

MONI: Shouldn't we call him?

SANDRA: I think we need to leave him alone.

MONI: Okay, but we're not going to bother him, we just want him to know we're with him during this moment, that's all.

SANDRA: I think if he needs anything, he'll call.

MONI: But since he didn't want to tell them what happened, they're watching him because he's missed work.

SANDRA: But if we don't tell them he's missed work, they're not going to find out. Are you telling them?

MONI: No.

SANDRA: Okay.

MONI: Okay, sometimes yes, if they show up and he's not here, what are we supposed to say? He's got us involved in this too.

SANDRA: Who knows... Fucking drawer.

MONI: I put your test results in the closet.

SANDRA: Good, thanks. Did you order some food?

MONI: No, they'll call in a bit for our order.

SANDRA: I'm starving.

MONI: Sandra...

SANDRA: What?

MONI: You know that you can count on me for anything, right?

SANDRA: Sure. Listen, the keys to the file room that were here?

MONI: In the third drawer. I put your keys on a ring, they were all loose.

SANDRA: What time did you get here?

MONI: Oh, I did that last night before I left.

SANDRA: Such dedication.

MONI: Sandy, are you going to let them see the one for the uric acid?

SANDRA: What?

MONI: Some of the levels came back wrong.

SOFIA: Phone.

SANDRA: Hello, yes, Sandra. (*To* MONI) Our food. What? No, nothing, the bus was late, that's all. What time I get here is my problem, I'll ask you not to interfere in my business, please, I have my own way of doing things, alright?

MONI: You can't show them these.

SANDRA: Are you going to get something to eat?

MONI: I'm not hungry.

SANDRA: Okay. What do you have for today?

MONI: Chicken, Sandra, they always have chicken, we're going to explode from all the hormones.

SANDRA: Garlic but no skin. And besides potatoes, what do you have? Okay, potatoes. Listen, the potatoes, can they be boiled? Boil them for me with just a squeeze of lemon. And the chicken cooked all the way through. Almost burned. Do you still have breast? Well, a thigh then. Send me some lemon, a lot, yes. What? Oh well, roast them... No, the potatoes without lemon then. Do you have mashed potatoes? Okay, roasted potatoes then.

MONI: A salad would be better...

SANDRA: You have any salads? Celery?

MONI: No, no celery.

SANDRA: Put in some celery, but no lettuce. Oh, it comes with the chicken? Okay then. No, take off the chicken with garlic and give me the chicken salad. No garlic, grilled, no eggs. Okay, put in an egg. Olive oil. Whatever you have, why give me a choice then? And some flan.

MONI: You think flan's a good idea?

SANDRA: No, she's not hungry. Okay, bye.

MONI: You know, I could eat a grilled sandwich…

SANDRA: Hold on, a grilled sandwich for Moni. We got cut off, they'll call back.

MONI: I'll just eat a little of yours…

SANDRA: My glasses' capace?

MONI: What's that?

SANDRA: The capace, the thing you store eyeglasses in.

MONI: It's called a "capace"?

SANDRA: Yeah, I dunno, I call them capaces, the ones that close up like a tube.

MONI: I didn't touch anything. I've never seen you with a capace.

SANDRA: Listen, if you're hungry, order something.

MONI: I'll just eat a little of yours.

SANDRA: No, don't eat off of mine, order what you want.

MONI: It's just that I don't know…

SANDRA: It's not that I don't want to share, it's just that afterwards we'll have to order again.

MONI: Their food's so heavy.

SANDRA: It's all there is.

MONI: Sandy, what are the test results for?

SOFIA: Phone.

SANDRA: Hello, we were cut off. Sorry, Hector, I thought it was the café. How are you?

MONI: Send him a kiss from me.

SANDRA: What? (*Pause.*) Hector's asking how can he tell if his mother's dead.

MONI: What?

SANDRA: I don't know... Is she breathing?

MONI: Tell him to call a doctor.

SANDRA: Did you call a doctor? So what did he say? Oh...

MONI: So?

SANDRA: Do you need anything?

MONI: Tell him to take the day off, we'll cover for him.

SANDRA: Yeah, sure.

MONI: Well, she's not suffering anymore, right?

SANDRA: No, nobody around here knows anything. No, she didn't say a word.

MONI: Ask him where the wake's being held.

SANDRA: Of course you're going to be able to, why wouldn't you?

MONI: Where's the wake?

SANDRA: Remember that you were always there for her.

MONI: Is there going to be a wake?

SANDRA: Don't you have any cousins who can help out?

MONI: He doesn't have anybody.

SANDRA: Don't worry.

MONI: Poor woman.

SANDRA: Take it easy, we both send you a kiss.

MONI: Ask him where's the wake.

SANDRA: A big kiss, bye.

MONI: Where's the wake?

SOFIA AND MANUEL'S HOME:

MANUEL: I could never have any kids.

SOFIA: Why not?

MANUEL: Because I couldn't...

SOFIA: Yeah, you already said that. But why not?

MANUEL: Because I can't imagine what I could give them so they'd be happy.

SOFIA: Nobody knows that. It's just desire, that's all.

MANUEL: Desire to do what?

SOFIA: To have a kid.

MANUEL: That's nothing. I imagine that somebody could suddenly feel he doesn't really want to have them anymore. That he never wanted to have kids. But there it is. There they are. And your life is with them, forever. And you begin to hate them because you can't get yourself free of them.

DOCTOR'S OFFICE:

SANDRA *seated behind the main desk, which now functions as a doctor's office.*

SANDRA: Sandra Rimabisius. How are you? Yes, I'm a bit late, sorry. I've brought the test results. No, he couldn't come, he got caught up at work at the last minute. But we didn't want to miss the appointment. Yes, we've been trying for some time, but no luck. He'll want to try some treatment too, it's just that today he got caught up. Yes, we've been trying for some time. On my family's side, no, but on his there's a history. Two aunts. I think the problem's coming more from his side. He had a bicycle accident when he was young. I think so. He has a scar... Yes, of course, we'll both come. Of course. With his test results. He already had them done, they're in his office. Is there anything I can start taking? Fine, nothing. Is next week good? Speak with the secretary, fine. Good bye. (*She leaves.*)

SOFIA AND MANUEL'S HOME:

SOFIA: You could never hate them. You might get tired. But you'll always love them.

MANUEL: How do you know?

SOFIA: I imagine.

MANUEL: Well, I imagine too. And since I don't know, I don't plan on making anybody suffer.

SOFIA: You don't know a thing. About anything in life. But you have desires too.

MANUEL: My desires are short-term.

OFFICE:

MONI's *never left the desk;* HECTOR *enters.*

MONI: Hector, honey, come here, give me a hug.

HECTOR: I wanted to come by even for just a little bit.

MONI: You did the right thing, what are you going to do at home with all those memories? Come here and sit down.

HECTOR: Marta's already left?

MONI: Who's Marta?

HECTOR: Sandra…

MONI: Oh… Sandra… she was up on five, photocopying. You want me to make you a sandwich? Tell me all about it.

HECTOR: Well… she… died.

MONI: How awful…

HECTOR: Yes.

MONI: At least she didn't suffer?

HECTOR: Well, the truth is she suffered a lot, yeah.

MONI: But why? Because of her illness?

HECTOR: Yes, of course. The sedatives weren't...

MONI: They weren't working anymore.

HECTOR: Right.

MONI: So she was aware of everything.

HECTOR: Yes, she never lost consciousness. And my stuff?

MONI: Sandra and I've been organizing things a bit.

HECTOR: Thanks for covering for me. I didn't want them to find out.

MONI: No worries. So tell me, did you get yourself checked out?

HECTOR: No, why?

MANUEL: Phone.

MONI: No, no reason. Don't think about that. (*Answering the phone*) Hello? Yes, he's here. (*To* HECTOR) It's the café.

HECTOR: Hello. Yes. Oh, thanks a lot. No, she didn't suffer. I wanted to come here to clear my head a bit. I figure I'll be back in the next couple of days.

SANDRA *enters*.

MONI: We have a visitor.

HECTOR (*on the phone*): No, seriously I'm not hungry, thanks for asking.

SANDRA: Hi, Hector.

HECTOR: Later. Thanks.

SANDRA: Hi, Hector.

HECTOR: How're you doing? Long time.

SANDRA: Fine. We didn't expect you back already.

HECTOR: I wanted to clear my head a bit.

SOFIA: Phone.

MANUEL: Yeah, yeah, the phone.

MONI: Hello. Yes, he's here. (*To* HECTOR) It's personnel.

HECTOR: They know too?

MONI: Something.

HECTOR: Hello. Yes. Thanks very much.

SANDRA: How is he?

MONI: Sounds like it was a nightmare. Poor thing. The sedatives didn't work.

HECTOR: No, she didn't suffer...

MONI: She suffered like hell right up to the end.

HECTOR: Just like she was asleep, yeah...

SANDRA: Poor thing.

HECTOR: Tomorrow I'll come back to work. I apologize for the bother.

SANDRA: Did you tell them?

MONI: Yes, I didn't have any choice.

HECTOR (*hanging up*): Good bye.

SANDRA: Would you like some coffee?

MONI: The machine's not working.

HECTOR: I don't want anything, I should be going.

MONI: Stay a bit longer. We'll keep you company.

SANDRA: Let him do what he wants if he wants to go...

HECTOR: No, it's okay, I'll stay a little while. My chair?

MONI: It's in accounting. One of theirs was broken and well...

SANDRA: Take mine.

MONI: I'll go look for yours.

HECTOR: Don't worry about it. It doesn't matter.

MONI: No, it's okay. I'll be right back.

MONI *exits. Silence.*

SANDRA: Want to do some work?

SOFIA AND MANUEL'S HOME:

MANUEL: You look at me as if you're always wanting something from me, and that makes me sick...

SOFIA: You take yourself too seriously. You think your take on the world's the most important. Your positions.

MANUEL: I don't have anything to offer anybody.

SOFIA: I don't take you seriously.

MANUEL: Are you listening to me?

SOFIA: Shut up, I'm getting tired. I don't take you seriously. I love you, that's all. That's why you can't stand me.

MANUEL: You don't know me.

SOFIA: You do everything you can to make me leave. Make me hate you, run away, make me think you're a terrible person.

MANUEL: You don't know me.

SOFIA: And you probably are. I'm sure you are. But you're not as bad as you think.

MANUEL: I don't have anything to offer anybody. Not even myself. I can barely breathe.

OFFICE:

MONI (*offstage*): Where are you going to go eat?

SANDRA: I don't know, he set it up.

MONI: Go somewhere important for you both. Where did you meet?

SANDRA: At my other job. Where I was before. (*She exits.*)

MONI: Cool.

SANDRA: What?

MONI: Meeting him at work.

SANDRA: Yeah.

MONI: And so... it happened there, in the office?

SANDRA: No, no.

MONI: You're too reserved. I can't get anything out of you.

SANDRA: It's just not that interesting. Are you done in the bathroom?

MONI: Yes…

SANDRA: So…

MONI (*entering*): How long have you been together?

SANDRA: Four years.

MONI: Four years?

SANDRA (*entering*): Yeah, married four years.

MONI: That makes it your… whatever… anniversary.

SANDRA: It's a lot, isn't it?

MONI: An eternity to me. Did he propose to you in the office?

SANDRA: I don't remember.

MONI: What do you mean you don't remember your own husband's proposal?

SANDRA: I don't know, he was filling in, he's a treasurer.

MONI: You were meant to meet, it was fate, right?

SANDRA: No, Moni, it was a fill-in. What's fate got to do with it?

MONI: I believe in those things.

SANDRA: Good for you, I don't.

MONI: But give me the details. Were you attracted to him from the start?

SANDRA: No. He wasn't exactly good-looking.

MONI: He wasn't your type.

SANDRA: Look at this perfume I bought last week, all the liquid's on top and the gel's on the bottom, it's not coming out… what a rip-off…

MONI: But tell me. I think deep down you're a romantic.

SANDRA: He'd just sprained his wrist while he was working in the office, so he couldn't write. And I had to write down everything he dictated to me.

MONI: That happened to me once, it's awful because they can't put a cast on it, you have to use a scarf, not even a sling.

SANDRA: He had a sling.

MONI: Then it wasn't a sprain, it must have been something else.

SANDRA: No, it was a sprain and he had a sling.

MONI: That doesn't sound right.

SANDRA: It depends on your doctor, some put you in a sling and others don't.

MONI: Okay, but don't go changing the subject. So then?

SANDRA: So he dictated, and I wrote it down.

MONI: On the computer?

SANDRA: Yes, of course. There were numbers and accounts and really technical words.

MONI: What did you tell me he was?

SANDRA: Treasurer.

MONI: How about that, a good-looking treasurer. All the ones I've ever met were scrawny.

SANDRA: So suddenly, right in the middle of dictation he starts telling me that he can't think because I'm there. That I'm inhibiting him. So I look up at him, but he says: "No, don't look at me, would you be so kind as to write it down." He was very formal then. Now, too. "Please write it down," he says, "it's dictation. From the first time I saw you last Tuesday in the file room, I cannot get you out of my mind. I think only of you. Day and night. Signed... your future husband."

CAFÉ – SOFIA AND MANUEL'S HOME – OFFICE:

HECTOR (*positioning himself to the left of the main desk, which now functions as a café table*): I've never been here before, it's very nice, tiny. Warm. I like that it has a bar. But it's better at this table. I don't know this area very well, I never come around here. Yeah, sure, I go out, but more around my own neighborhood... downtown. I work around there too. So I don't get out of the neighborhood much. Everything's right there. You know I really liked it when you smiled, when I first got here. You have a really pretty smile. Serious, too. You're really pretty today. You're really pretty. Sure, go ahead, I'll wait.

SANDRA (*using the phone on the desk, right, her back to the audience*): I'd like to make an appointment. Tuesday at 6, great, not a problem. No, I'll be on time, don't worry. Do we need to bring any test results? Okay, great. That's all. We'll be there. Wait, I have another question. Are you going to do anything to me? I don't know, you tell me... Wednesday then. Tuesday? Tuesday. No problem.

HECTOR: Yeah, the women's bathroom is always too small. You want to leave? Hold on, I want to ask you something. Do you have your own place? Yeah, I live alone, but... it's kind of embarrassing. I really like you. And I'd really like to. But at my place... there's still my mom's furniture, she died just a little while ago. And I never took anyone back to my place when she was alive. And I want to get rid of her stuff, but it's kind of hard. And until I get rid of it... I'm 51. Yeah, I know. It's not you.

SOFIA: You're a monster?

MANUEL: Yeah.

HECTOR: ... immature, yeah.

SOFIA: You're a little boy?

MANUEL: Yeah.

HECTOR: ... Oedipal, I understand.

SOFIA: You're a saint?

MANUEL: Yeah.

HECTOR: I understand. Let's be honest, sure.

MANUEL: We're not going anywhere, you and me.

HECTOR: ... I understand you perfectly. Sorry to have made you come all the way out here.

SOFIA: Let's stay in.

OFFICE:

They're putting on their coats to leave.

MONI: And this bag?

HECTOR: Nothing. I'm going.

MONI: Show me. What…? Are you afraid of me?

SANDRA: What I don't understand is… are they going to do it all by e-mail? Don't they send letters anymore?

MONI: No. It's all by e-mail. Be sure to bundle up.

HECTOR: It's free.

SANDRA: But with e-mail you don't know if the other person got it, with a letter if it doesn't arrive it gets returned.

MONI: Exactly. All that has its price.

HECTOR: What about us then?

MONI: I don't know…

SANDRA: They're going to come up with something. They'll move us to another section.

MONI: If we're lucky. Shall we go?

SANDRA: Why?

HECTOR: Did you hear something?

MONI: Every so often they cut back on personnel. If they're not mailing letters, why would they want us around?

SANDRA: But they're not going to fire us, are they?

HECTOR: Supposedly they can't fire us.

MONI: You know how everything around here can change in a minute. Put your coats on so we can go downstairs.

HECTOR: My dad worked here for forty years, and they used to move him from one place to another but they never fired him.

SANDRA: Supposedly they can't.

HECTOR: I mean, I think there are laws. They can't. Unless they change them, but… they've been around for a long time. The laws, I mean. I don't know if they can change them. In order to fire us. But first they have to change them. I don't know if the president changes, he can change the laws. I don't know if they're laws or habits or decrees. We should ask.

MONI: Sure…

HECTOR: I'll head down soon. You go on. See you tomorrow.

MONI: What are you still working on?

SANDRA: Leave him alone…

MONI: Suddenly now he's decided to work.

HECTOR: I have a few things to get ready for tomorrow.

MONI: Need any help?

HECTOR: No, no thanks, you go on.

SANDRA: Let's go, I don't like going down the stairs by myself.

MONI: Good thing there wasn't anybody inside. Imagine. You'd kill yourself.

SANDRA: Do you have a lighter?

MONI: Yes.

SANDRA: Use it to light up the stairs.

They leave.

HECTOR *stays behind; he's anxious about something. He takes a stylish jacket out of the bag and puts it on. He combs his hair. He takes a piece of paper out of his pocket, opens it, sits down in the armchair, and picks up the phone.*

SANDRA *comes back in.*

SANDRA: Excuse me, Hector, I forgot a file.

She sees him.

SANDRA: I've got a doctor's appointment tomorrow and if I don't take this file…

She doesn't know if she should say something. HECTOR *looks at her.*

SANDRA: I'll let you go. See you tomorrow.

She doesn't know if he wants to say something.

SANDRA: You need anything? You okay?

HECTOR: Can I ask you a question?

SANDRA: Sure, of course.

HECTOR: Tell me the truth.

SANDRA: What's up?

HECTOR: How does this jacket look on me?

SANDRA: Good.

Pause.

HECTOR: How's my hair?

SANDRA: Good. Different.

Pause.

SANDRA: Anything else?

HECTOR: No. Thanks a lot. Sorry.

SANDRA: Don't worry about it.

SANDRA *is about to leave.*

HECTOR: Can I ask you one more question?

SANDRA: Yeah, sure.

HECTOR: Do you like this better or the way I usually dress?

SANDRA: This is good. But before wasn't bad either.

HECTOR: Understood.

Pause.

SANDRA: Can I go?

HECTOR: I wanted to ask you one more thing.

SANDRA: Sure, tell me.

HECTOR: Please don't be offended.

SANDRA: Don't worry.

HECTOR: If you don't want to, you don't have to answer.

SANDRA: Tell me, don't be afraid.

HECTOR: Do you have the feeling you could ever fall in love with me?

SANDRA (*uncomfortable*): Oh, I don't know, Hector, I've never thought about it.

HECTOR: No, not you in particular. I mean anyone, could someone ever fall in love with me?

SANDRA: Why not?

The electricity goes out.

SANDRA: Stop, Hector, don't move… Hector… I really value our…

The lights come back on, and MONI *is standing in the doorway.*

MONI: Wow, that was scary. What are you two still doing here?

SANDRA: I forgot a file.

MONI: Oh, your tests. I left my house keys. What an idiot. And on top of that, those stairs… This place is gonna kill me. What with the cold and the workout… Where are they? What are you…? Do you have your appointment tomorrow?

SANDRA: No. Yes.

MONI: Did you find it?

SANDRA: What?

MONI: The file.

SANDRA: Yes.

MONI: Ah. My keychain, my keychain… what if no taxis came by, or what if I took one and I only noticed when I got home I didn't have my key. (*To* HECTOR) Did you finish yet?

HECTOR: Yes.

SANDRA *would like to talk some more.*

MONI: You two go on, I'll keep looking.

SANDRA (*to* HECTOR): You want to go downstairs?

HECTOR: No, we'll help you look. Where could they be?

MONI: How would I know… you two go on.

SANDRA: I'm going down, how about you?

MONI: Go on, kiddo. You'll be stuck here until I find them.

HECTOR: Sure?

MONI: Yeah. They have to be in one of these drawers.

HECTOR: Are these the ones? (*They're hanging from* MONI'*s purse.*)

MONI: Where were they?

HECTOR *indicates the purse.*

MONI: How embarrassing. Sorry…

SANDRA: At least they showed up.

HECTOR: Yes.

MONI: What a dummy… Are you both ready?

HECTOR: I am.

SANDRA: Me too.

MONI: Okay, let's go.

SANDRA: Yes. (*To* HECTOR) Do you have a lighter?

MONI: I do.

SANDRA: Use it to light up the stairs.

HECTOR: Careful. Slowly.

SANDRA: Lucky nobody was in the elevator, huh?

HECTOR: How far did it fall?

SANDRA: From the third floor.

HECTOR: Thank goodness.

MONI: Anyway we're prepared. Right? What's there to lose?

SOFIA AND MANUEL'S HOME:

MANUEL *stands up and moves across the space as if to leave.*

SOFIA: Where're you going?

MANUEL: Out for a walk.

SOFIA: I don't believe you.

MANUEL: Then don't ask.

SOFIA: Do whatever you want, but I'd rather know.

MANUEL: Really?

SOFIA: Yes.

MANUEL: I'm going out for a walk.

SOFIA: Wait. Are you really attracted to him?

MANUEL: No.

SOFIA: Are you more attracted to him than to me?

MANUEL: No, he's ugly.

SOFIA: What do you need? What do you want me to do so you'll stay
    with me?

MANUEL: I need something else.

SOFIA: So what does he do for you?

MANUEL: Freaks me out.

SOFIA: And what do I do for you?

MANUEL: Bring me down.

DOCTOR'S OFFICE:

SANDRA *enters and goes over to the main desk, which once again serves as a doctor's office.*

SANDRA: Sorry, there was a demonstration and all the streets were barricaded, I'm very sorry. I brought the test results. Look, we have a problem. My husband doesn't want to come. He doesn't believe in this. He says that if he has to give you some semen, he'll do it, but he doesn't want to talk with you or any other doctor, or take any tests. I already told him. But since he has children from his first marriage, he says that he's not the problem. And if you agree to, let's tell him where he has to give… the… sample, and you and I can carry on with our business. Oh, I understand. I'll call you then.

OFFICE:

MONI *and* HECTOR *enter.* SANDRA, *who's remained seated at the desk, begins to take off her scarf and jacket.*

HECTOR: Does this toothbrush belong to one of you?

MONI: No.

HECTOR: That's weird, it wasn't here yesterday.

MONI: It must be the cleaning people, give it to me and I'll take it to them.

SANDRA: Anyway we need to say something, yesterday I found some Maxipads in the wash basin. And the floor was wet. It seems to me that since the lock's broken, these people are using the place to bathe.

HECTOR: But how are they going to bathe in cold water?

SANDRA: Well, they're people who don't have anything. They probably don't have water at home.

MONI: But how are they going to bathe here?

SANDRA: I don't mean to judge, but they should do it in the kitchen or someplace else. Who knows what we'll pick up in the bathroom afterwards. Have you gotten some sun lately, Hector?

HECTOR: No.

SANDRA: You look tan.

MONI: Hey, they left Güiraldes's thermos here. He committed suicide so now they're handing out his stuff. Do we want it?

SANDRA: It gives me the creeps.

MONI: But we'll rinse it out.

HECTOR: And his family didn't take it?

MONI: No, it gave them the creeps too.

SANDRA: How awful. It's still warm.

MONI: No, I put some water in to see if it worked. Since they were giving it away, I figured it was broken.

SANDRA: I'd rather not. I'm not superstitious but… I don't know, he used to drink out of it.

MONI: But this way we'll have a thermos, which isn't bad.

For some time HECTOR *has been sitting in front of the typewriter.*

SANDRA: Why don't you use the computer?

HECTOR: The mouse isn't working.

MONI: You can use the keys: F1 and Enter to scroll down, F2 and Enter to scroll up.

SANDRA: And to click?

MONI: Hit Control-Alt and without releasing, Enter plus F3.

SANDRA: That's impossible. What do you have to do?

HECTOR: It's been two months since Mom's passing, and the family always holds a mass. Since they couldn't come to the burial, everyone's coming to the mass.

MONI: Now they show up?

SANDRA: Don't butt in.

HECTOR: No, it's that her sisters from back home are all old and in order to travel they have to plan ahead. They can't just up and go. I understand.

SANDRA: So what do you have to do?

HECTOR: I should say a few words in front of everyone, and the thing is I don't really know. Stand up there. And talk. I don't know what'll come out.

SANDRA: Well, don't talk if you don't want to.

MONI: But it's good for him to talk since it was his mother.

SANDRA: But if he doesn't want to…

HECTOR: No, it's not that I don't want to. I'm afraid that in the moment…

MONI: You'll cry.

HECTOR: No, if I cry, I cry. But I don't know if I'm going to know what to say.

MONI: So write it down.

HECTOR: Sure. That's why I wanted to use the computer.

SANDRA: Oh, and it's not working.

MONI: Use the typewriter.

HECTOR: Yeah, that's what I'm…

SANDRA: Do you want me to help?

HECTOR: No, thanks. I think it's something I have to do myself.

SANDRA: Did they leave anything else to give away?

MONI: The jacket he was wearing, they didn't want to take that.

SANDRA: No way.

MONI: No, anyway accounting took it. I think it fit him.

SANDRA: No way I'd put it on.

MONI: Well, you can't let the bastards get you down, otherwise…

SANDRA: Did his secretary take it really hard?

MONI: Yeah, because it all happened so suddenly. Poor guy, he was just about to retire.

SANDRA: God only knows what was going on with him.

MONI: Loneliness. He lived for his job, and he had nothing now that he was about to retire.

SANDRA: But something more must have been going on.

MONI: Well, yeah. His wife had died. And he hooked up with some broad who took everything he had. She even got him to put his house in her name. His oldest son got a depressive disorder after his mother's death and ended up half-mongoloid, on medication. And he has two other sons, one with some rare virus that's eating up his skin, he's in the hospital. And the other one helped out his father, but they didn't get along. Because it seems that he couldn't forgive him for losing the house to that girl. In short, a shitty life. What was he going to do? Good for him.

SANDRA: What did you say?

MONI: No, not good for him, but I understand.

HECTOR's *made a few attempts at typing but throws the page away.*

MONI: What's the matter? Nothing's coming out?

HECTOR: The truth is, no.

SANDRA: What do you want to write down?

HECTOR: Well, talk about her.

SANDRA: Right. Talk about nice things.

HECTOR: Yeah, it's not the time for reproaches, is it? Ha ha.

MONI: What was your mom's name?

HECTOR: Susi. Her name was Susana, but everyone called her Susi.

SANDRA: So start with that. Today we're remembering Susana who was Susi to all of us.

MONI: But you should say something about the day. That's being commemorated.

SANDRA: That it's been a month?

HECTOR: Two months.

MONI: Exactly two months?

HECTOR: Yes, because we wanted to do it on a Sunday when it's free, but it fell on a Wednesday so now we have to pay for the mass. But everyone wanted to do it at exactly two months. Family custom.

MONI: Okay. Write that you've come together today for the two-month anniversary, that it's been exactly two months since she died.

SANDRA: Not since she died, since she ceased to exist, right?

MONI: We've come together today to… celebrate's not right…

SANDRA: Commemorate…

MONI: Remember…

SANDRA: Commemorate…

MONI: To commemorate that two months ago she ceased to exist…

SANDRA: Susana ceased to exist, known to all of us as Susi.

MONI: It's not that she ceased to exist, that's the physical disappearance. But her spirit or the memory we all have of her is still here present in all of us.

HECTOR: So what do I put down then?

MONI: That.

SANDRA: Something like… Do you want me to write it out?

HECTOR: Yes, please. I'm really slow.

SANDRA: I'll do it by hand and we can type it up later. So…

MONI: It's exactly two months today since the disappearance of the body but not the spirit of Susana, known to all of us as Susi…

SANDRA: Known to all of us as Susi.

HECTOR: Her sisters called her Ñuca.

MONI: Why?

HECTOR: Don't know, something from when she was a kid…

SANDRA: Fine. We can put down all the nicknames she had.

MONI: Ñuca, her sisters called her.

SANDRA: Known to her sisters as Ñuca. What else? What did her nieces and nephews call her?

HECTOR: Aunt.

MONI: No, aunt's very common.

SANDRA: But if they called her aunt, you're not going to write something else. Known to all of us as Susi, to her sisters as Ñuca, to her nieces and nephews as Aunt.

MONI: Put auntie, it's more personal.

SANDRA: Nieces and nephews as Auntie. Afterwards we'll recopy it.

MONI: Any other nickname?

HECTOR: I don't know, let me think…

MONI: Grandma? Did she have grandchildren?

HECTOR: No, she would have loved it, but…

SANDRA: So no Grandma.

HECTOR: Nobody called her Grandma. Everyone in the neighborhood called her Carmen, because she didn't like Susi so she had them call her Carmen.

SANDRA: Known to the neighborhood as Carmen.

MONI: But will anybody from the neighborhood be there?

SANDRA: What does that have to do with it?

HECTOR: Yes, somebody certainly will be there, they loved her a lot.

SANDRA: What else?

HECTOR: I don't know…

MONI: We're going to remember her. Remember her as she was. As she was in life. So that her memory can live on.

SANDRA: Let's keep her memory.

MONI: Let's preserve her memory.

SANDRA: Preserve?

MONI: Yeah, that's better, isn't it?

HECTOR: Yeah, let's preserve is better.

SANDRA: I'll take out keep and put in preserve. Afterwards I'll copy it over. What she meant. What does everyone remember?

HECTOR: Well, she was a really good cook.

SANDRA: The memory of her meals.

HECTOR: Empanadas.

MONI: Are you going to go into detail?

SANDRA: That's good about the empanadas. What else?

HECTOR: No, she mostly made empanadas.

SANDRA: Her empanadas, period.

Silence.

HECTOR: Animals. She really liked animals.

SANDRA: Should I write her love?

MONI: The love she was able to give to us as well as to animals.

SANDRA: Do you like that?

HECTOR: Yeah, that's good. 'Cause she was affectionate.

MONI: And that he's going to carry on her… what do you call it? Not her insignia, her good name.

SANDRA: What do you mean by that?

MONI: That Hector's going to carry on her legacy.

SANDRA: And legacy.

MONI: Legacy's good.

SANDRA: And I will carry on. No…, I will transmit.

MONI: I will transmit the legacy of everything she did for all of us and for the animals.

SANDRA: I think that's enough with the animals.

HECTOR: Yeah, I think mentioning them is…

SANDRA: I will carry her legacy…

MONI: Forth…

SANDRA: I already wrote that. Legacy…

HECTOR: So you'll always be proud of me.

MONI: No, I think that makes her look like she pressured you.

HECTOR: No, I'd like to tell her that she'll always be proud of me.

SANDRA: I think Moni's right. It looks like she wasn't proud.

HECTOR: But she was proud.

MONI: Okay, then there it is. Everyone knows she was proud.

HECTOR: Yeah, right. But let's say it.

MONI: I wouldn't put it in, but it's your mass.

HECTOR: What do you think?

SANDRA: I don't like it much.

HECTOR: Okay. Then no. Let's leave legacy and that's it.

MONI: With much love. Your son, and you're set.

SANDRA: Thank you for everything is better.

MONI: I don't know. Hector, you decide.

HECTOR: Thank you for everything. I think that's good.

SANDRA: Thank you for everything, Susi.

MONI: Hector. Susi's the one being honored. Hector signs.

SANDRA: Fine, but include her name. Thank you for everything, Susi.
   Hector.

MONI: That's it. You like it?

HECTOR: Yes. Thanks a lot.

MONI: Take the paper with you and read from it.

DOCTOR'S OFFICE:

SANDRA, *who's already seated at the main desk, simply looks forward.*

SANDRA: Doctor, I need to tell you something. I know. I arrived late,
   but I couldn't… I apologize. Yes, it matters to me. I couldn't get
   here earlier. I work, you understand? Yes, I apologize, it's not your
   problem. Doctor. I want to tell you something. I'm very ashamed.
   I lied. I don't have a husband. Did you figure it out? I never did.
   Well, yes, almost, just for a short time. But it's been years since I've
   seen him, I don't know anything about him. The point is I lied. I'm

alone. I'm running out of time, and I want to have a baby. It's the thing I want most in the world. And I don't care if I have to have it alone. I don't care whose child it is. Afterwards I'll raise it myself. Can't you help me get pregnant? (*Silence.*) I'll leave the test results. And, please, don't discuss this with anyone.

CLUB:

HECTOR's *in one corner of the space, talking in a loud voice like he's in a club.*

HECTOR: Hi, yes, what's there to drink? Huh? A beer, please. I pay over there? And then come back? Great. What's your name? I said, what's your name? I don't understand. I come back here after and order the beer. (*He turns around.*) Where's the cashier? So I can pay for the drinks. The cashier. What? What? Okay, thanks a lot. What's your name? I said, what's your name? Sorry, I don't understand. Where? Over there? But now I'm supposed to take the ticket for the beer over to that guy. We can leave afterwards if you want. I said I have to go pay for the drinks. At the cashier. Afterwards I'll go order it over there, and then we can go. You want me to look for you over there? Okay. What's your name?

SOFIA AND MANUEL'S HOME:

MANUEL *enters.*

SOFIA: Let me help you. What happened to you?

MANUEL: Nothing, leave me alone.

SOFIA: It's okay if you don't tell me, but let me help you. You're hurt all over. Did they beat you up?

MANUEL: Yes.

SOFIA: Why? I was scared, I called your folks and they didn't know anything. Be sure to call them later, they're worried.

MANUEL: You're a moron, why did you call them? How would they know?

SOFIA: What did I know, last time you went to their place.

MANUEL: Don't worry about me, don't follow me. Didn't you say that you didn't care? That I could come and go, isn't that right?

SOFIA: How am I not going to care if I don't hear anything from you for three days? What if something happened to you?

MANUEL: You have this way of making it so that the more you do for me the more I hate you. (*Pause.*) Forgive me. Don't believe me when I talk to you like that. I thought I was going to die. I was sure they were going to kill me. I was afraid for the first time in a long while. And at that moment I missed you so much. I wanted you to be there with me. I love you.

SOFIA: I love you too. You've never said anything like that to me before.

MANUEL: Yes. I want to be near you when I die.

During the following scene, MONI *takes a small blanket out from under the armchair, sits down, and goes to sleep.*

CLUB:

In the same place as before.

HECTOR: Oh, hi, you can't see a thing in here. What's your name? Do you always come to this place? It's my first time. I'm not used to the noise. You can't see a thing in here. I feel a little old for this place. Yeah, I live alone. No, there's no problem. It's near here. Yeah. Anyway, I have to go to work early tomorrow. If it doesn't bother you. Let's go then. What's your name?

OFFICE:

SANDRA *enters silently and finds* MONI *sleeping. She doesn't say anything.*

SOFIA: Phone.

SANDRA: Hello, yes, no, I'm a little hoarse. No, there's no one here yet, I'll let you know.

HECTOR *enters.* SANDRA *motions to* MONI, *but* HECTOR *does not respond. He goes over to his desk. Silence.*

SANDRA: Hector.

HECTOR: What?

SANDRA: Don't you ever want to have a child?

SOFIA: Phone.

HECTOR: Phone.

MANUEL: Phone.

The telephone wakes MONI *up.*

MONI: Sorry. Sorry. I can explain.

HECTOR: Hello. Yes. How did you get my number? No, I'm working now. You can't stay at my house. Get out before the neighbors see you. Hold on a sec...

HECTOR *changes phones.*

SANDRA *(to* MONI*)*: Don't worry.

MONI: It's just that I finished up late last night... Hi, Hector.

SANDRA: Don't worry about it. Your toothbrush is in the bathroom.

MONI *leaves for the bathroom.*

HECTOR: No. It's just that I wear that jacket. We can go look for another one together if you want. I'll call you. Don't call here. Later. Leave the keys. Bye. Bye. (*Hangs up.*) What were you saying?

SANDRA: Nothing, forget about it. Moni woke up. Moni, are you okay?

MONI: I'm really sorry. I don't know how to make it up to you. I'll be right back...

She exits and comes right back in.

MONI: I lost my place, and the thing is I can't bother my family anymore. I thought that if it didn't bother you, I'd pick up everything in the morning. It's just for a while, that's all.

HECTOR: All right. Let's get to work now.

SANDRA: Can I help you? Some people are coming by.

MONI: No, no, I'll pick up. I'll put on my shoes and pick everything up. I swear I'm desperate. I thought a lot about it. I already lived at my cousins'. But they have families. And I swear that I helped out, kept things in order. I cooked for them so I wouldn't be a burden. But sure, they have their own lives. That's why I stayed here. I don't like it either.

SANDRA: All right. It doesn't bother me. Hector, does it bother you?

HECTOR: Not me. If you're comfortable with it.

MONI: I'll go as soon as I find another place. Please let me know if you hear of anything. Any corner, even if it's a mattress on the floor. Hector, I don't know if your house, your mom's room… or Sandy, if you have any room at your place. I know that your husband's left, maybe a bit of company would do you some good. I don't have any privacy here. I'm going to the bathroom.

SIMULTANEOUS SCENES:
SOFIA AND MANUEL'S HOME – CAFÉ – RESTAURANT – CAFÉ:

Four different scenes take place simultaneously in the same area, with the characters in their respective locations: SOFIA *and* MANUEL *are at home,* HECTOR *is in a café,* SANDRA *is in a restaurant, and* MONI *is at another café. The dialogues should lightly overlap.*

HECTOR: Order whatever you want. Don't worry. You're hungry. Why don't you ask them to wrap it up so we can take it home? That way we're more relaxed.

SANDRA: Sorry I'm late. Nice place.

HECTOR: You could've called me no matter what. That way I wouldn't worry.

SANDRA: I'm all sticky. From running to get here.

HECTOR: I bought you this t-shirt. Let's see if you like it…

SANDRA: I left home thinking it was going to be cold and then… What are you drinking?

HECTOR: You can exchange it anyway. It's just next door to my place. They have everything.

MONI (*entering*): Excuse me. Is this the smoking section? Where is it? It's just that it's kind of cold to be outside.

HECTOR: 84 when she died. But she was great.

SANDRA: What do you eat here? Pasta?

HECTOR: She took care of the house, everything…

SANDRA: Salad?

HECTOR: She'd have dinner waiting for me. Every night.

MONI: A cup of coffee, please.

SANDRA: Let's see.

HECTOR: Sometimes I'd eat out and then have to eat again because otherwise she'd get offended.

SANDRA: Do you have artichokes? How do you prepare them? Do they have a lot of seasoning?

HECTOR: A bit of everything...

MONI: Thanks a lot. No, nothing else.

HECTOR: High blood pressure, lots of scarring, diabetes...

SANDRA: Potatoes. Yams. Green beans. Are the beans fresh?

SOFIA: Time!

MANUEL: You bitch, how do you do it?

SOFIA: Country, Denmark.

HECTOR: Three cracked ribs, two herniated discs...

SANDRA: And could you gratinée them after? Just a bit. Don't burn them.

MANUEL: Go...

SOFIA: Time.

MANUEL: "G."

HECTOR: It's not easy to change out the furniture. It's really expensive.

SANDRA: Well. Here we are.

HECTOR: Yes. Order whatever you want.

SANDRA: So... what's new? It's been a long time. You look great.

HECTOR: It's just that I don't know anything about you. I've told you everything and you...

MANUEL: Me what?

SANDRA: You're not the same, but it suits you, age, I mean.

HECTOR: Sometimes I can't tell if you're having fun when we're together.

SOFIA: Gingivitis.

MANUEL: What's that?

SOFIA: A disease.

MANUEL: Doesn't count. Nobody knows what that is.

SOFIA: I had it.

MANUEL: I don't know...

SOFIA: You also have...

MANUEL: I don't think it counts.

HECTOR: So what do you do?

SANDRA: No, I've had my stories but nothing very earth-shattering...

SOFIA: But you always end up making your own rules.

HECTOR: But what do you like to do?

SANDRA: Tell me about yourself. Are you with anyone?

SOFIA: Okay. Go ahead. Fine. Now you start.

SANDRA: Good for you...

MANUEL: Go...

SANDRA: A bunch.

HECTOR: Do you have any brothers and sisters?

SANDRA: Do you have any kids?

SOFIA: Time.

MANUEL: "P."

HECTOR: I would have liked to have had brothers and sisters. Share the load, right?

SANDRA: All girls?

HECTOR: Not because of my mom.

SANDRA: Oh. I'm so sorry.

HECTOR: Because of everything in general.

SOFIA & MANUEL: TIME!

MONI: My coffee's gotten a little cold. Could you heat it up for me?

HECTOR: I want to tell you something.

SANDRA: I called you for a reason.

HECTOR: I tried to get close…

SANDRA: This may seem strange to you, in your situation.

HECTOR: Stuck. No future.

SOFIA: What are you thinking? Your face's changed.

HECTOR: There's an age. Or a time in life.

SANDRA: There's a time in life when…

MANUEL: I don't know if I want to say…

SOFIA: Oh?

HECTOR: But for me it's important.

MANUEL: Not for me.

SOFIA: Better if I shut up?

MANUEL: Yeah.

HECTOR: Let me speak.

SANDRA: I'm sure if you compare it to you and your wife, I guess ours was just a brief moment.

MONI: Oh, thanks a lot. It's nice and warm.

HECTOR: If it's going to be like that. I'd rather we didn't see each other anymore.

SANDRA: Yes.

MANUEL: No.

SOFIA: Yes.

SANDRA: I got over it. It's not that.

HECTOR: Yes.

SOFIA: Yes.

MANUEL: No.

SANDRA: But you were important to me.

MANUEL: Yes.

SOFIA: Really?

HECTOR: No. I would've loved to, but it couldn't be.

MANUEL: No?

SANDRA: I would like you to be the father of my child.

HECTOR: No.

SOFIA: No.

MANUEL: No.

MONI: No, no.

SANDRA: I'm not asking you to see it afterwards. Or support it.

MANUEL: No.

HECTOR: I hope you find someone who understands you.

SANDRA: What is it you don't understand?

MANUEL: What is it you don't understand?

SOFIA: Why don't you go to hell, you idiot!

She leaves.

SANDRA: What is it you don't understand?

HECTOR: I don't like to yell or fight.

SANDRA: Ridiculous.

HECTOR: I just can't do it.

SANDRA: I think it's the least you could do after disappearing like you
    did.

HECTOR: I don't think so. I think it's best to cut things off completely. There it is.

SANDRA: What does it cost you? It's my time of the month. You understand?

HECTOR: Bye, Manuel. It was really nice knowing you.

SANDRA: Come on. Just a little while tonight and I won't bug you ever again. I swear.

HECTOR: I'll pay, leave it.

SANDRA: Right. All forgotten. We never talked about it.

HECTOR: Lots of luck.

SANDRA: It's done. No need to explain. Get the check and we'll go. What? Okay… What did I get? A salad. Isn't the price there?

HECTOR: Bye. Be good.

He leaves.

SANDRA: Okay, but you drank too. Let's split it. Okay. I had the salad. The soda. And half the wine. Do they charge for the bread? So split it if you want. Flan. Extra for the whipped cream? How much is the cream? And the coffee. Two cups, you're right. Tell me how much it is, please, so we can get out of here.

MONI: The check, please. Thanks.

OFFICE:

MANUEL: May I…

MONI: Strange he hasn't shown up yet. He's usually very punctual.

MANUEL: Not a problem, I can wait.

MONI: That's his desk. Here's another girl, Sandra, who usually arrives later. And I move around from one desk to the other.

MANUEL: What's this office for?

MONI: What do you mean what's it for?

MANUEL: I mean… what do you do here?

MONI: Before we used to do all the... but now since they don't send letters anymore. I don't really know what they're going to do with us.

MANUEL: Weird, huh?

MONI: Yeah. There's nobody else left in this wing of the building. In the first wing and the second one, yeah, but not here... I don't know why they leave us here.

MANUEL: They probably forgot.

MONI: Yes, maybe, hmm? Ha. Has it been a long time since you saw Hector?

MANUEL: Yeah, a bit.

MONI: He's probably changed a lot then.

MANUEL: Yeah, sure.

MONI: Are you on his mother's side or his father's side?

MANUEL: Father's.

MONI: That's good, because you know his mother died, right?

MANUEL: Yeah, I knew.

MONI: Well, his father died too, but that was a long time ago.

MANUEL: Is he in a relationship now?

SANDRA *enters*.

SANDRA: Sorry I'm late.

MONI: Don't worry, there's nobody left in personnel. (*To* MANUEL) They moved them to another building.

SANDRA: Hi, how're you doing?

MONI: This is Manuel, Hector's nephew on his father's side.

SANDRA: How about that...

MONI: Yeah. He never told us anything. He's going to be happy to see you.

MANUEL: Yeah.

SANDRA: Did the phone come back on?

MONI: No. And I didn't call to find out. Because it's not working.

MANUEL: So...

MONI: You asked me something, excuse me...

MANUEL: If Hector was in a relationship or something like...

SANDRA: Moni, can you come over here for a second, please.

MONI: Excuse me for just a second.

SANDRA: I don't have a problem with you staying here, but don't leave your leg wax around, it's disgusting.

MONI: But are you using this box?

SANDRA: What does that have to do with it?

MONI: That's fine. I didn't think it was going to bother you.

SANDRA: So you think...

MONI: Coffee?

SANDRA: Sure.

MONI: Manuel?

MANUEL: Okay.

MONI: The water's already hot.

SANDRA: I brought some sugar. (*She pulls some of the café's sugar packets out of her purse.*)

MONI: Manuel, can you help me with this lid? It's really stuck and I can't get it open.

MANUEL: Are you sure Hector's coming in today?

MONI: He didn't call to say he wasn't.

SANDRA: How can he call if there's no phone.

MONI: Well, then, I don't know...

HECTOR *enters, his hair dyed black.* MONI *stands in front of* MANUEL *so* HECTOR *can't see him.*

HECTOR: Hi. Got held up, I apologize.

SANDRA: Don't worry. We haven't started yet.

His new look shocks the rest.

MONI: Did you have to take care of some paperwork?

HECTOR: No, no.

MONI: Because sometimes... paperwork can drag on.

SANDRA: Hector.

HECTOR: What?

SANDRA: Something's different about you.

HECTOR: Oh, yeah. Thanks.

SANDRA: You're welcome.

MONI: A lot better, huh.

HECTOR: Thanks. Is that coffee I smell? Any left?

MONI: Yes, it's ready. Help yourself.

HECTOR *gets up and goes over to* MONI.

MANUEL: You want milk?

HECTOR: Hi. How're you doing?

MANUEL: I don't know. Looks like you're doing really bad.

HECTOR: Hmm. If you like, we can go get coffee somewhere quiet.

MONI: You're not bugging us here...

MANUEL: I'm great here. Does it bother you?

HECTOR: No, I mean, so we can talk quietly.

SANDRA: Moni, can you help me take these files to the archives?

MONI: But there's nobody...

SANDRA: Doesn't matter. We can leave them by the door.

MONI: Okay. Let's go.

HECTOR: No, you stay. We can go instead.

MONI (*to* HECTOR): It's no problem if you two want to talk, Sandy and I'll go down to the café.

HECTOR: Sandra, let's not get behind in our work. You two get started. I'll be back in a while.

SANDRA: Sure? Whatever you want.

HECTOR: I think that's better.

MANUEL (*on top of* HECTOR's *line*): What, you're afraid of being alone with me?

MONI: We better go, Sandy…

SANDRA: No. How are we going to go?

HECTOR: Let's talk quietly. You think?

MANUEL: No, I don't think. I think that you're a liar. That's what I think.

HECTOR: Calm down.

SANDRA: Please…, what's your name?

MANUEL: Manuel.

SANDRA: Please, Manuel, why don't you let Hector go and we'll have our coffee?

MANUEL: Why don't I bust your face, that way I don't have to listen to you?

MONI: I'm calling the police.

MANUEL: You stay right where you are, or I'll hurt him. I mean it. Understand? Stay nice and quiet.

MONI: What should I do, San?

SANDRA: Stay still, moron.

MANUEL: So you thought you could disappear just like that. That I wouldn't find you?

HECTOR: I thought that was clear the last time.

MANUEL: Clear for you. Nothing was clear to me.

SANDRA: What do you want? Money? I have some, take it.

HECTOR: No, Sandra. Don't worry.

MONI: I have a little bit too. Not much but…

HECTOR: Don't worry, it's something else.

SANDRA: We'll give you what we have and then you'll go.

HECTOR: Shut up, you two. Don't get involved. If I say he doesn't want any money, he doesn't want any money.

MONI: Okay, sorry. We were just helping out.

MANUEL: So you do know how to raise your voice? Suddenly you're all macho.

MONI: Did he tell you about any family problems?

SANDRA: Shut up, Moni.

MANUEL: What I don't understand is if you dyed your hair to be better looking or so I wouldn't find you…

HECTOR: Wait, please.

MANUEL: Answer me.

HECTOR: What?

MANUEL: Did you dye your hair to be better looking or so I wouldn't find you?

HECTOR: To be better looking.

MANUEL: Well, look at you. (*To the women*) So did it work? Is he better looking? Answer me.

MONI: Well, yeah.

SANDRA: Different…

MANUEL (*to* SANDRA): Tell the truth or I'll kill him.

SANDRA: Sorry, Hector, but the truth is no. That color looks terrible on you.

MONI: But he just did it. You have to wait for it to settle…

MANUEL: You don't have the right to leave anybody, understand? You don't have the right.

SANDRA *grabs him from behind, they struggle.*

SANDRA: Look, dumb-ass. You're a little young to come around bullying three people who are working. I don't want to hurt you, so lower the decibel level so we can talk.

MANUEL *pins her against the wall.*

MANUEL: Do they know you were fucking me all this time? (*Silence.*) You wanted me to talk. I talked.

HECTOR: No, I didn't want you to.

SANDRA: Hector, I never imagined.

MONI: And with your own nephew.

HECTOR: We never talk about these things.

MONI: That's true. Privacy is privacy. You don't have to share if you don't want to.

HECTOR: I would have told you, but the opportunity never came up.

MONI: We thought you were being weird. Different, I mean.

SANDRA: You know that I don't understand you either?

HECTOR: How so?

SANDRA: The truth is I feel a little deceived, Hector. Sorry, but that's the truth.

MONI: Yeah, me too, it's logical, but it's nothing serious.

MANUEL: Who do you think you're kidding? I used to listen to you scream all night long.

MONI: Please, there's no need.

SANDRA: I suddenly have the feeling I don't know you. I thought we trusted each other, you even talked to me about stuff.

HECTOR: What stuff?

SANDRA: Love, Hector. You talked to me about love. Or maybe I misunderstood.

HECTOR: You misunderstood. Because I...

MONI: Excuse me, but I'm kind of confused.

MANUEL: What?

MONI: Are you his nephew or what?

MANUEL: No, why?

MONI: Well, you told me…

MANUEL: I lied.

MONI: Oh, okay, I just wanted to know.

HECTOR: You've got to understand that it wasn't easy for me to talk about this either.

SANDRA: Why?

HECTOR: I didn't know how you would take it.

SANDRA: What do you think we are?

HECTOR: I don't know…

SANDRA: That your private life matters to us… Give me the glass, Moni!

MONI: Okay, I've got it in my hands… (*Pause.*) But, are you in love with him?

MANUEL: Does it look to you like I could be in love with this guy?

MONI: So?

HECTOR: Moni, where's the glass?

MONI: You want to drink something? I'll serve you, I keep it hidden here so they don't find it…

SANDRA: Did he talk to you about love and other stuff?

MANUEL: Yeah. He loves me.

SANDRA: He loves you.

MANUEL: He told me so.

MONI: Did he tell you so too, San?

SANDRA: I don't know…

SOFIA *enters.*

HECTOR: I've never loved anybody, I don't understand what's going on…

MANUEL *(bears down on him)*: What did you say? What are you saying? Tell the truth, tell me you love me…

SANDRA: Please, help us.

MONI: He's threatening us…

MANUEL: What're you doing here?

SOFIA: Let's go, Manuel.

MANUEL: What're you doing here?

SOFIA: Come on, let's go home.

MANUEL: Are you following me?

SOFIA: Yes. Leave the gentleman alone and let's go home. I don't know what you're doing, it doesn't matter to me, but it's not good for you. Leave the gentleman alone and let's go home.

MANUEL: Were you listening?

SOFIA: No.

SANDRA: She just came in.

HECTOR *(to MANUEL)*: Who's she?

MANUEL: None of your business.

SOFIA: I apologize. I don't know what he did to you, but I swear it won't happen again. Let's go.

MANUEL: You go to hell. I'm not leaving with you.

Pause.

SOFIA: Is this the guy?

MANUEL: Yeah.

SOFIA: What's your name?

MANUEL: Shut up.

SOFIA: It's just a question. What's your name?

SANDRA: Don't answer.

SOFIA: And who are you?

SANDRA: What's it to you?

MONI: We work here, we're Hector's coworkers.

SOFIA: Hector? Your name's Hector?

SANDRA: Sorry, Hector, I shouldn't judge you…

MONI: Sorry, Hector.

SOFIA: So this is the guy who hit you?

HECTOR: What?

SOFIA: Is it?

MONI: You hit him, Hector?

MANUEL: Yes.

HECTOR: No. How could I hit him?

SANDRA: I really don't understand anything now. My God, Hector. Who are you? Who are you??

HECTOR: I never hit him. He told me his partner hit him.

SOFIA: That's what you told him?

MANUEL: Can you leave? You've already busted my balls. And now you're following me around too?

MONI (*to* SANDRA): She must be the girlfriend.

SANDRA: Keep your voice down.

HECTOR: Are you his girlfriend?

SOFIA: Yes.

MONI: But she's a woman…

SANDRA: Yes…

SOFIA: Yes…

MONI: No… you're cute…

SANDRA: Could you go over there to the other side, please? I don't want you talking to me.

MONI: Okay. It looks like we're all really worked up.

SOFIA: He dyes his hair, Manuel.

MANUEL: He dyed it today.

MONI: Yes. That's from today. His hair is usually ash-colored.

SANDRA: Listen up, Monica. There's a limit between your life and the lives of others—do you understand?

MONI: What're you talking about?

HECTOR: Calm down, Sandra.

SANDRA: Somebody has to tell her. We're not interested in having you butt into our lives, and, Hector, I apologize for speaking for you.

HECTOR: No, it's not okay.

SANDRA: Shut up. Read a book, make up your own world, whatever, but just let the rest of us live. I'm sorry I said all that, it's not true. Sorry. Sorry.

MONI: Do you think the same way, Hector?

HECTOR (*shrugging his shoulders*): Well...

SOFIA: What's going on with you? What's going on in your head? My God. Help me understand you. I can't take it anymore. I don't know if I should commit you. Or leave you alone so you can kill yourself. I don't know. What are you looking for?

HECTOR *tries to console* SOFIA, *but she pushes him away.* SOFIA's *now standing in front of* SANDRA. *Pause. She hugs* SANDRA.

SANDRA: Calm down. Come, sit. Moni, let's give her the chair, she doesn't feel good. (MONI *gets up.*) You want some coffee? Moni, can we make her a cup?

MONI: There's no more coffee, we ran out.

HECTOR: You want some water?

SOFIA: Yes, please.

SANDRA: Will you bring us some water?

MONI: Go and get it yourself. I'm not butting in anymore.

HECTOR *goes in search of water.*

MANUEL: Are you sick? You want some water? Hector's very nice, he's going to get you some water.

SOFIA: I swear he's unbearable. I can't take it anymore.

SANDRA: Calm down. It can't be that serious.

SOFIA: It's not that he's unbearable. I'm unbearable. I can't stop loving him and he's a son of a bitch. He can't love anybody.

HECTOR: I understand.

SOFIA: What do you know? What can you know about him?

HECTOR: Not much, that's true. But I loved him.

SOFIA: Really? (*Silence.*) How does everyone else do it? How do they do it? (*To* SANDRA) Are you married?

SANDRA: No.

SOFIA: You have any children?

SANDRA: No.

MANUEL: Let's go home. Come on.

SOFIA: No, I'm not going anywhere. Don't you want me to talk? What's wrong with you?

MANUEL: I don't want you to act like a fool.

SOFIA: Me act like a fool? You go to bed with this older guy with dyed hair. Hey, sorry… and I'm the one acting like a fool? You think it matters to me if I act like a fool?

HECTOR: It's just the first day…

MANUEL: I know I was bad. Let's go.

SOFIA: Ask the gentleman to forgive you.

HECTOR: No, it's not necessary.

SOFIA: Ask him to forgive you.

MANUEL: Me?

SOFIA: Yes.

MANUEL: Forgive me, Hector.

SANDRA: Let's go. Tomorrow we'll feel better and we can talk. If we need to talk.

HECTOR: I don't know how everyone else does it.

SANDRA: Okay. Tomorrow we'll talk more calmly. (*To* MONI) Whatever's said in a situation like this doesn't count.

HECTOR: Let's talk tomorrow.

Pause.

MONI: But tomorrow's Saturday, you're not coming in.

HECTOR: Right. (*Pause.*) Monday, Monday we'll talk.

Pause.

SOFIA: Tomorrow's not Saturday, tomorrow's Thursday.

HECTOR: Thursday?

SANDRA: Of course, today's Wednesday.

Pause.

MONI: Today's not Friday?

MANUEL: No, today's Wednesday, tomorrow's Thursday.

Pause.

HECTOR: Of course, today's Wednesday.

SANDRA: Yes. If yesterday was… well, okay.

MONI (*laughing at* SANDRA): It's just death getting closer and making us all stupid. Right?

Pause.

MANUEL: Let's go?

Pause.

SANDRA: So, yes, tomorrow we'll come and talk calmly.

HECTOR: Okay.

Pause. MANUEL goes over to SOFIA and kisses her. She takes him offstage.

MONI: Did you say the mass for your mom, Hector?

HECTOR: No… in the end, no…

Pause.

HECTOR: Weird, huh?

SANDRA: What?

HECTOR: Well… everything…

MONI: Yes… it's true.

SANDRA: Yes…

Pause.

MONI: You want to order some food?

SANDRA: No…

HECTOR: No…

Pause.

MONI: The phone's not working anyway…

The office's phosphorescent light starts to flicker. Blackout.

END OF PLAY